THERAPY GAMES FOR TEENS: EASY AND PRACTICAL CBT AND DBT TOOLS

MANAGE ANXIETY, DEPRESSION, AND STRESS, IMPROVE COMMUNICATIONS SKILLS AND SELF-ESTEEM THROUGH FUN ACTIVITIES

TABLE OF CONTENTS

INTRODUCTION

Play is essential for a teen's healthy brain and nervous system growth. A teen's capacity to self-regulate, form social bonds, and acquire executive function skills are all affected. It's how they learn about the world, interact with people, find solutions to problems, grow as individuals, find their voice, and convey what they need. The benefits of play extend well beyond childhood because it is based on our primal selves. For play therapy, the most important thing is to have fun.

In play therapy, you are encouraged to be goofy and have fun. It's true that "laughter is the best medicine," but it's not the only reason this is an effective therapy. For example, our ability to relate to others improves when we are allowed to play about and be ourselves without the burden of expectations for perfection. And as we form secure bonds with others, we can better access the regions of our brains that are damaged and in need of repair.

When conventional treatments have failed, we may find relief via play therapy. Under stress, our brain may switch into "protective mode." The thinking part of our brain, which engages in the kinds of executive functions and task management needed to deal with the demands of everyday life, like following directions and sitting still, is unavailable to us when we are in this state.

For instance, the "thinking brain" is the only one typically used in Cognitive Behavioral Therapy. But if we have trouble switching on our analytical faculties, no amount of "thinking it out" can help us alter our actions.

Furthermore, we can sort through our complicated emotions and develop strategies for overcoming obstacles through playing, a process that essentially sidesteps our logical brain.

HOW TO USE THIS BOOK

There is a significant difference between therapeutic play and play therapy that needs to be clarified before using this book. When a therapist uses therapeutic play, the goal is to help the client heal from a traumatic experience, overcome generalized anxiety, increase the client's ability to manage emotions, improve family dynamics, boost self-esteem, or address other specific psychological needs. Of course, the kind of unplanned play parents do organically with their children can also satisfy these requirements.

In contrast, play therapists actively guide clients toward these outcomes.

Therefore, it is important to clarify that this book is not a replacement for actual play therapy and should not be regarded as a treatment for disorders like ADHD or PTSD (PTSD) .—(Does " PTSD" have to be written twice?) However, any caring adult should encourage their teen to participate in the planned play activities presented in this book. Teens are discouraged from playing in today' s society for various reasons, including increased screen time and shorter recess periods at school. This book will assist you in reintroducing your teen to the play necessary for healthy development.

This book includes fun and simple activities that have been carefully selected to appeal to a wide range of teenagers. However, not every teen will enjoy the same activities. Your youngster can benefit from slowing down with some activities while getting a boost of energy from others. Because you know your child better than anyone else, it' s up to you to decide which experiences are ideal for them at this stage in their development.

CBT

This book also addresses various clinical conditions and diagnoses by integrating the core components of Cognitive Behavioral Therapy. Each activity will include a focus on comprehension, healing, and restoration. The first step is analyzing one' s ways of thinking and behaving to meet the particular challenges posed by a specific issue.

While we may have to repeat certain methods, each set of exercises will focus on a unique clinical issue and incorporate new, evidence-based practices. The methods will also guide you to other activities from various chapters to expose you to a wide range of evidence-based strategies.

For you to make real gains, regular practice is essential. Get in the habit of practicing newly acquired competencies daily or weekly until you have mastered them. Please do not rush through the exercises. Feel free to review any exercises you' ve completed, whether you found them easy or challenging. Most people will benefit most by beginning each chapter, working through the first exercise until they have mastered it, and then moving on to the next activity.

You may not need to employ every single CBT technique. Instead, it would help if you choose exercises you feel the most comfortable with. You should be encouraged to apply your judgment. You can use these as a handout in class or send them home as homework. When used for practice outside of therapy, teens might be reminded of the significance of consistency if (– should " if" be " in" ?) an exercise.

Regardless of your lack of familiarity with CBT, you and your teens will find helpful information in this book. You or your teen's ability to choose which exercises to Implement within a given portion will depend on your assessment of the teen's condition.

DBT

Those who have attempted Cognitive Behavioral Therapy (CBT) and other treatments without success should read this book. How we were raised and the circumstances we were exposed to as children profoundly impact our personalities and responses to life's challenges. If this book does anything, I hope it is to reassure you, dear reader, that you are not alone. Anxiety, depression, and overwhelming stress affect millions of people, and there is a wide range of severity. Your current emotions may make you incredibly isolated, but you are not.

There are places you may go to get help if you or someone you know is experiencing a crisis. If you are feeling overwhelmed, it is recommended that you seek immediate assistance by calling a loved one or researching local crisis hotlines online. We can move forward if you feel ready to take charge of your issues. To get the most out of this book, read it chapter by chapter and do the activities after each chapter. Then, you may read the material repeatedly until you understand it completely.

Remember that it's important to take your time with each chapter. The same is true for life in general; some days will be easier and more fruitful than others. And you'll want to take a break every once in a while. So refresh yourself and take a break when that happens.

It takes a lot of energy to deal with worry and help yourself. You must confront your past, your emotions, and the activities that seem both physically and mentally difficult. However, there is one cardinal rule I insist upon. PLEASE TREAT YOURSELF WITH KINDNESS. Make this phrase the wallpaper on your computer or phone, post it on your bathroom mirror, and put it everywhere as a constant reminder to treat yourself with compassion and forgiveness.

However, it's important to remember that you are more than the sum of your experiences and your parents' or caregivers' parenting styles. By picking up this book and committing to better yourself, YOU ARE INCREDIBLE.

You should be proud of this initial step!

In this session, we will go over some DBT exercises. You should still go through the chapters and the exercises even if you haven' t been diagnosed with anything. Those who don' t suffer from OCD could nevertheless gain from doing the DBT exercises in that section. In addition, anyone suffering from anxiety or conditions associated with anxiety, such as phobias, social anxiety, PTSD, or attention deficit hyperactivity disorder (ADHD) , can benefit from dialectical behavior therapy (DBT) .

We appreciate your effort and want you to know that you are not alone in this journey.

Part 1: Adolescence

Chapter 1: Definition of Adolescence

Adolescence is the phase of life between childhood and adulthood, from ages 10 to 19. It is a unique stage of human development and an important time for laying the foundations of good health.

Adolescents experience rapid physical, cognitive and psychosocial growth; This affects how they feel, think, make decisions, and interact with the world around them.

Despite being considered a healthy stage of life, there is significant death, illness, and injury in the adolescent years. Much of this is preventable or treatable. During this phase, adolescents establish patterns of behavior – for instance, related to diet, physical activity, substance use, and sexual activity – that can protect their health and the health of others around them or put their health at risk now and in the future.

To grow and develop in good health, adolescents need information, including age-appropriate comprehensive sexuality education; opportunities to develop life skills; health services that are acceptable, equitable, appropriate, and effective; and safe and supportive environments. They also need opportunities to meaningfully participate in designing and delivering interventions to improve and maintain their health. Expanding such opportunities is key to addressing adolescents' specific needs and rights.

Adolescence is a time of growing independence when you begin to question your parents' authority and seek your path in life. This process may be quite a task, especially when weighed against the myriad other demands placed on kids today: academics, social obligations, romantic commitments, extracurriculars, jobs, parties, and dealing with the new normal of drug use and sexual promiscuity.

Adolescence is a stage of maturation marked by the pursuit of new interests, the formation of new connections, and the tentative testing of previously unknown waters. You are in an ideal position to acquire these skills as a teen while still developing and discovering who you want to become. In addition, completing the tasks in this book will have gained you wisdom and understanding that most people don' t gain until much later in life, if at all.

5

CHAPTER 2: ASPECTS OF ADOLESCENCE

Early adolescence, often ages eleven to fourteen, middle adolescence, ages fifteen to seventeen, and late adolescence, ages eighteen to twenty-one, broadly split the adolescent years between puberty and adulthood. In addition to physiological development, seven important intellectual, psychological, and social developmental tasks occur during these years. The basic objective of these tasks is to prepare for adulthood and the formation of one's identity.

PHYSICAL DEVELOPMENT

Adolescence's biological changes constitute puberty. By mid-adolescence, if not earlier, most children have completed their physiological growth; they have reached or are close to their adult height and weight and are now physically able to have children.

INTELLECTUAL DEVELOPMENT

Most boys and girls start puberty still understanding the world in dichotomous terms: things are either right or wrong, great or terrible. Younger adolescents' failure to comprehend the long-term effects of their activities stems from the fact that they rarely look beyond the present.

By late adolescence, many adolescents have developed an appreciation for the nuances of circumstances and ideas and the ability to predict the future. Their ability to solve difficult problems and perceive what others are thinking has greatly improved. However, because they are still relatively inexperienced in life, even older adolescents may employ these newly acquired skills haphazardly and act without consideration.

PSYCHOLOGICAL DEVELOPMENT

Besides sleeping late on weekends and cleaning out the refrigerator, if teens can be said to have a purpose, it is to express their independence. But, of course, this requires that they separate themselves from their parents. The march toward autonomy can take various forms, including less overt affection, more time spent with friends, argumentative conduct, and pushing the boundaries.

Nonetheless, adolescents usually feel ambivalent about leaving the protection and security of their homes. They may oscillate between wanting your attention and withdrawing from you.

SOCIAL DEVELOPMENT

Until now, a child's existence has mostly centered on the family. As a result of adolescence, her social circle expands to include friendships with individuals of the same sex, the opposite sex, various social and cultural groups, and other adults, such as a beloved teacher or coach. Teenagers eventually acquire the ability to fall in love and build romantic relationships.

Not all teens begin and exit adolescence at the same age or exhibit the same characteristics. Moreover, throughout most of adolescence, a child may be better developed in some areas than others. However, it is not until late adolescence that intellectual, emotional, and social development begins to catch up with physical development. For example, a fifteen-year-old girl may physically resemble a young adult, but she may behave like a child.

Given that society places adolescents in a state of limbo for six to ten years, is it any wonder that they occasionally feel confused and conflicted? Before World War II, around one in four adolescents completed high school. It was normal to be employed full-time, married, and have children. Almost three-quarters of today's students graduate from high school, with two-fifths continuing to college. The age range of adolescence has been extended into the twenties, according to Dr. Joseph Rauh, an expert in adolescent medicine since the 1950s. "As more and more adolescents have continued their education," he explains, "the age range of adolescence has been extended into the twenties."

Consider your teenage years, and you may recall the frustration of desiring independence yet still being financially dependent on your parents or seeking to be your individual while also desiring to fit in with your peers.

Even for parents, adolescence can be bewildering. They must, for example, struggle with their children's frequently contradictory behavior. How is it that the same son given to arias about preserving the rainforest must be frequently reminded to sort the recycling? Or, in an hour, your daughter can accuse you of treating her "like a baby" and then look insulted when you ask her to clear the table after dinner?

In addition to learning to anticipate the shifting currents of adolescent mood, however, moms and fathers may be experiencing their own conflicted feelings. The satisfaction you experience as you observe your child gaining independence can be tempered with a feeling of displacement. As much as you may understand that a child' s withdrawal from their parents is a natural part of growing up, it still hurts when the youngster who used to beg to accompany you on errands no longer wants to be seen with you in public.

It' s reassuring to know that experiencing a sense of loss is a common reaction that' s probably shared by half the soccer moms standing next to you. As pediatricians, advising and guiding parents constitutes a significant and rewarding portion of our day.

While entering adolescence may be daunting for you and your child, recognizing the ups and downs of each developmental stage helps better equip you to face any obstacles. As described by the American Academy of Pediatrics, you may generally anticipate the following changes during the three stages of adolescence. Each stage is divided into separate lists of physical and mental/ emotional developments.

10 TO 13 YEARS OLD: EARLY ADOLESCENCE

GROWTH AND PHYSICAL DEVELOPMENT

• During this period of adolescence, puberty begins for many children and pre-teens;

• pre-teens experience both physical growth and sexual development, which can be unsettling for them and teens.

• During early adolescence, the body may acquire hair beneath the arms, and in the pubic region, testicles may enlarge in males, and breasts may develop in girls.

• Changes typically begin earlier in females than in males. In most circumstances, girls may begin developing a year or two before boys.

• Changes can begin as early as eight years of age in girls and nine in males but become more pronounced during the onset of adolescence.

MENTAL AND EMOTIONAL GROWTH

• As pre-teens and adolescents progress through adolescence, they begin to claim greater independence; this implies kids may rebel, particularly if their parents enforce rules and establish restrictions.

• Often, children of this age have a greater demand for privacy, which indicates their desire for greater independence and less supervision.

Additionally, they may need greater seclusion to manage the curiosity and anxiety accompanying body changes and new emotions.

•During this stage, children may become aware of their gender identity or begin to question it; this may last throughout the adolescent years.

•It is usual for pre-adolescents to become more self-centered or selfish. Their self-centered ideas and emotions cause individuals to be self-conscious.

•At this point, children begin to feel like they are always being assessed by others, particularly their classmates.

•At this stage of adolescence, youngsters have a fairly binary way of thinking. Something is either correct or incorrect, with no possible alternative interpretation. Infrequently they view things as merely " okay."

14 TO 17 YEARS OLD: MIDDLE ADOLESCENCE

PHYSICAL DEVELOPMENT

Teens continue to undergo puberty-related changes during middle adolescence.

• Physical changes in females may have slowed or ceased by this age, but most will begin menstruating regularly.

• The majority of boys will have begun their adolescent growth spurt.

• Male voices begin to become softer, and there may be a phase in which they crack.

• Acne occurs in both men and women.

MENTAL AND EMOTIONAL GROWTH

• During this stage, while the brain develops, cognitive processes mature but do not yet function like an adult's.

• The frontal lobes are the final regions of the brain to mature and are not fully developed at this point. The frontal lobes are responsible for complicated decision-making, judgment, impulse control, and considering the repercussions of actions. They are capable of using logic but are largely motivated by emotion.

• At this age, adolescents develop an interest in romantic and sexual interactions.

• It is typical for people to investigate their sense of self, beliefs, and values. Some adolescents desire to blend in with their peers, while others wish to assert their uniqueness.

AGES 18 TO 21: LATE ADOLESCENCE

PHYSICAL EVOLUTION

For most adolescents, physical growth is complete by late adolescence. Most individuals have reached their full adult height.

MENTAL AND EMOTIONAL GROWTH

During late adolescence, the maturation of the brain is complete. However, the frontal lobe does not mature until approximately age 25. Therefore, some individuals consider the ages 18 to 24 late adolescence.

• Typically, adolescents in this age group have greater impulse control and decision-making abilities than those in middle adolescence. Risks and rewards are analyzed more precisely.

• Older teenagers have a heightened sense of self-identity.

• During this stage, values, and beliefs are generally solidified.

• Young people's independence increases as many move out of their parent's houses.

• Thoughts may move to the future, and actions may be based on their ideas, desires, and hopes.

• Relationships with parents, siblings, and other family members may transition as they approach maturity.

Chapter 3: Issues that Modern Adolescents Face

3.1 Anxiety

Anxiety is defined by feelings of fear or unease that are triggered by stimuli that provide no genuine danger. Several different physiological and mental symptoms represent anxiety. First, anxiety is a state characterized by an excessive and unwarranted fear of negative consequences in everyday life.

Anxious tendencies could be genetically predisposed. Family members may serve as a model for using anxiety as a coping mechanism. There are many ways in which our bodies react to stress. Anxiety and fear are learned responses to recurrent threats that might develop in someone who is chronically stressed: Age, experience, gender, their surroundings, the nature of the precipitating event, and the individual's traits all shape how someone reacts to a given scenario.

Feeling anxious is a normal reaction to pressure. The anxiety of a milder variety manifests as a generalized sense of unease and a marginal acceleration of heart rate. When anxiety levels are moderate, the individual focuses solely on the source of their distress, excluding anything else. Severe anxiety is characterized by recurrent periods of extreme stress and fear that build to a peak in minutes (panic attacks) . You can feel like death is imminent, have trouble breathing, experience chest pain, or experience irregular heartbeats.

What are the Signs of Anxiety?

Adrenaline and cortisol, two stress hormones, are released into the bloodstream as the body prepares to deal with the stressor. The body's stress reaction involves the shutdown of unnecessary systems and the activation of others in preparation for either a fight or a flight. The digestive process slows down, which can cause symptoms including coughing, dry lips, and nausea.

If your heart rate accelerates, your blood pressure will rise. In addition, increased heart rate and blood flow to the muscles might cause you to feel tense or anxious, make you sweat heavily, and cause a red face or other physical manifestations of heat; this is because you begin to breathe more rapidly to help obtain enough oxygen for the muscles to run away.

Anxiety typically manifests itself through an imbalance of four major neurotransmitters (chemical messengers in the brain) . It is believed that an imbalance of these neurotransmitters contributes to the development of anxiety when we are under stress. Dopamine activity is increased in anxious patients because serotonin and GABA levels are low.

Adrenaline secretion rises right after a traumatic occurrence. What exactly does this mean? When GABA is not there to dampen the activity of the other neurotransmitters, stimulation occurs. Anxiety and sadness are more likely to arise when serotonin and dopamine are overstimulated (and not controlled by GABA) . More dopamine in the brain can make us more susceptible to unpleasant and racing thoughts.

There is a higher likelihood that we may exaggerate the significance of a minor issue at this time, turning a molehill into a mountain. Adrenaline, which thrills the brain and body, exacerbates the symptoms and reduces our capacity for reasonable thought.

How Does Anxiety Affect Teens?

Anxiety can prevent adolescents from taking advantage of life' s opportunities, harming their growth and development. In addition, teenagers who suffer from persistent anxiety often report feeling lonely and helpless as they struggle to break the vicious cycle of obsessive-compulsive thinking and behavior.

If you suffer from anxiety, you likely had a period in your life when your coping mechanisms were temporarily impaired. After a trigger is triggered, you may be left with sensations of dread and panic. If your anxiety is giving you everyday stress, you should talk to your primary care physician about treatment options. If you don' t treat your anxiety, it can get worse, along with whatever underlying illness you have that makes you more vulnerable to stress.

How is Anxiety Managed?

The first step in altering our thinking is becoming aware of the thoughts that make us feel uneasy or undermine our confidence. When we recognize the ideas holding us back, we may take the first step toward changing those beliefs by bringing them into conflict with our rational thinking; this is an effective method for overcoming negative or distressing thoughts.

Identify Troubling Situations/ Conditions

Identifying your triggers is the first step. To begin, you may want to take stock of how you' re currently dealing (for example, by drinking to numb your feelings, bingeing to relieve stress, lashing out at others, or avoiding the issue altogether) . Once you' ve found the coping strategy, you may look for antecedents. What brought you to the point where you needed a beer? What/ who are you feeling the need to escape? Keep a notebook in which you record your findings so that you may track your development as a learner.

Become Aware of Your Thoughts

When you realize what set you off, write down exactly what happened. Pose some inquiries to yourself. What occurred? When it happened, who was I with? At what point did I realize I was starting to feel emotional? Where exactly did it occur? You can identify your triggers by analyzing the circumstance in terms of the who, what, when, and where. Reread your diary entry once you' ve finished the activity. Take note of and write down any reflections on the event that occur to you while you read. Doing this will aid in the identification of your habitual, disruptive ideas.

Identify Negative/ Inaccurate Thinking: Keep your emotions in mind during this introspection.

How intense is that feeling? How do you feel? Please use the 1-10 scale (1 is not emotional while 10 is highly emotional) . Don' t forget to keep track of how strongly you felt those emotions. There are occasions when you may feel a range of emotions. The emotions you feel after getting cut off in traffic and narrowly avoiding an accident, for example, may include both anger (at being cut off) and terror (of potentially being injured in a collision) .

Reshape Negative/ Inaccurate Thinking

Reframing your emotion is the next step. Here, you' ll brainstorm potential new approaches to the problem at hand. In the traffic scenario, for instance, you might tell yourself something like, " I almost got struck, but I am a skilled driver, and I was able to prevent an accident. I want to express my gratitude." Writing down your revised thinking is a good idea. Follow this procedure for each emotionally charged encounter you have documented.

Reread and Re-rate Your Thoughts

Finally, you should reread it and give it a new emotional rating. Once you have changed to several different feelings, it is helpful to revisit your initial feelings by reading about them again. The next step is to give them new ratings. Emotional intensity typically decreases, sometimes dramatically.

Practice makes perfect, so keep at it! Your automatic thoughts will also shift to be more optimistic as you grow more adept at altering your emotions.

3.2 DEPRESSION

Those who suffer from depression are afflicted with profound and ongoing feelings of despair. Sadness is a normal aspect of being human, but clinical depression lasts for long periods and interferes with daily life. A depressed person' s physical health, mental state, and thought processes may all suffer. Because of this, you' ll start to perceive things in a new light. It alters your mood, appetite, and social interactions. As a mental illness, depression is challenging to manage alone.

Teenagers with depression aren' t just feeling low or unwilling to " snap out of it." Long-term treatment, including medication and therapy, is often necessary for those suffering from depression.

In terms of depression, there are three distinct categories.

- Melancholy, which means " great sadness," is the first category. Unless treated, it can have a very long duration. People with depression have trouble emotionally and physically.

- Bipolar disorder, commonly known as manic depression, is the second form of depressive illness. Major mood swings are a possible side effect. When one feels happy and outgoing one minute, that individual may feel down and distant the next. Psychosis and the perception of non-existent sounds or objects can occur in extreme cases.

- Several distinctive symptoms characterize Dysthymia. Usually starting in childhood, this type of depression can linger untreated for decades.

WHAT ARE THE SIGNS OF DEPRESSION?

Sadness brought on by depression might last for days or weeks at a time. It makes you lose interest in things that used to matter to you. One' s inability to function normally or emotional fragility are not indicators of weakness or inadequacy in a depressed individual. It' s a serious medical condition that needs to be treated by a doctor.

The National Institute of Mental Health (NIMH) characterizes major depression as a condition that lasts for at least two weeks and significantly impairs everyday functioning. Sadness, anger, guilt or worthlessness, changes in eating, difficulties sleeping (or excessive sleeping) , low energy or weariness, and even thoughts of death or suicide can all be symptoms of depression.

How Does Depression Affect Teens?

Lack of appropriate guidance and support increases the likelihood that you may resort to harmful coping techniques.

Self-Harm

People often resort to destructive or risky actions because they have no choice but to do so to feel in charge of their lives. Someone who feels emotionally helpless in a certain area of their life may, for example, strive to gain control by regulating their bodily actions. Self-injury by cutting has become increasingly common among teenagers, which can be particularly challenging for parents. Many folks are misinformed and believe that cutting indicates a desire to die, whereas it only means that the person wants to give themself agony.

Some youths engage in less severe forms of self-harm, like beating themselves, punching walls, ripping out hair, etc. However, even if these harmful activities temporarily alleviate symptoms, the benefits won' t last. A person' s desire to self-harm may increase when the initial relief wears off. Self-harm is damaging and can lead to a cycle of negative behavior that is difficult to break.

Seeking Guidance from Peers and Social Media

Some teens attempt to cope with their issues by connecting with others who share common struggles. Social media and the Internet can be great places to find people with interests or relate to the same problems. But they can also be places of misguided information and uninformed individuals giving bad advice.

On the one hand, all humans are eager for connection, and social support can be a wonderful thing during times of stress or sadness. Technology opens doors to tons of people we may not otherwise meet, and it feels safe because of the anonymity it can provide. On the other hand, it has its dangers, and it' s important to be cautious when taking advice from people who are ultimately strangers and potentially just as stuck as you are. It' s easy for a teen who feels isolated and utterly alone at school to turn to online groups or others who seem to relate, especially if they' re the only places they feel like they can fit in or seek advice on how to feel better.

Sex, Drugs, and Alcohol

Teens struggling with depression, anxiety, or low self-esteem sometimes get overly involved in potentially risky things or seek pleasure that distracts them from their pain. Typical teenage experiences like sex, drugs, and alcohol can spiral out of control when they are used as a means to escape.

Peer pressure can be difficult to navigate when you lack the confidence and self-assurance to say " no." Turning to drugs or alcohol—or acting promiscuously to gain approval and acceptance—can lead to devastating consequences that only derail your chances of feeling happy and disrupt your progress in building self-esteem.

Disordered Eating

Disordered eating is another pattern rooted in control that can lead to serious consequences that require medical attention. Teens who feel powerless when facing their overwhelming, negative emotions might focus on eating and exercise as a way to regain some sense of control. Unfortunately, although dieting or exercise may start innocently enough, you can start to feel obsessive about the sense of control.

Things can rapidly spiral downward into serious eating disorders that are life-threatening and require intensive treatment programs to overcome. If you have been engaging in disordered eating or are struggling with body image issues, find a qualified professional to help you get back on a healthy track.

Avoiding or Masking

For some, avoiding, dwelling on, or drawing attention to the problem may be the only way they know how to deal with confusing or negative feelings. On the other hand, faking happiness and self-confidence may work temporarily, whether through extreme measures like bullying others or just putting on a happy front.

But in the long run, avoidance of the issues only makes them grow worse. In reality, when there is a difference between what people show the outside world and what they feel on the inside, it can cause them to become depressed. Part of building self-esteem involves being honest with yourself about your true feelings and developing the courage to make changes.

How is Depression Managed?

Treatments exist for depression. Early detection increases the likelihood of a successful outcome. A medical professional can diagnose your ailment and recommend a course of therapy. Cognitive Behavioral Therapy and antidepressant medication are the two mainstays of treatment for depression. Stress can be better managed, social interactions can be strengthened, and the individual's outlook can be boosted with the help of therapy.

Antidepressant medications. Change the electrical and chemical messages that are sent to the brain.

Cognitive therapy. Improvement in quality of life for depressed individuals. It will help the person relax, sleep better, have more energy, interact with others, and think more optimistically. Methodology centers on engaging in pleasurable pursuits that boost mood. If it works, you'll feel better and be able to put unpleasant ideas to rest.

Doctors can prescribe medication to aid patients with issues like low mood, low energy, and anxiety. However, it's time to consider switching to something else when a prescription medicine doesn't alleviate a patient's symptoms. (These medicines have any impact when taken as directed by a doctor.)

Whenever you notice signs of depression, it is best to get professional help immediately. A person's way of life will suffer as a result. If neglected, it can worsen to the point that recovery to a healthy mental state is nearly impossible. According to a recent WHO research, an estimated 350 million people worldwide experience clinical depression or seek medical help for it each year. For every 100 people, there are four who are depressed. Consequently, about 4.6% of the global population is affected by depression.

3.3 Stress

When we are overtaxed or no longer in familiar environments, our bodies react with stress. It can spur us on to greater efforts or paralyze us with inertia. Adolescence is when a person is constantly pushed to the edge of their comfort zone by various experiences.

Adolescents can harness the positive effects of this strong response by learning stress management techniques. They can learn to cope with adversity and embrace new challenges without giving up or giving in to despair.

WHAT ARE THE SIGNS OF STRESS?

As a result of stress, you maybe:

- Easily angered, frustrated, or tense
- Overwhelmed or overburdened
- Concerned, worried, or scared
- Feeling as though you can' t calm your mind down
- Unable to take pleasure in anything
- Depressed
- Disinterested in living as though one has lost one' s sense of humor
- Creeping dread
- Tensed up with worry
- Abandoned or alone
- Substantiated mental illness is becoming more dire
- Extreme stress might bring up suicidal thoughts in some people.

There are numerous physiological implications of the stress hormones our bodies generate. A few of the possible outcomes are listed below.

- Problems breathing
- Anxiety attacks
- Pain or blurriness in the eyes
- Disturbed sleep
- Fatigue
- Pain in the muscles and the head
- Heart palpitations with hypertension
- Acid reflux or indigestion
- Digestive issues, either constipation or diarrhea

- Feeling nauseous, lightheaded, or faint

- Extreme fluctuations in body weight

- Experiencing skin irritation or a rash

- Sweating

- Alterations in your menstrual cycle

- Chronic health issues; In other words, things are becoming worse.

These bodily impacts may further magnify in the presence of extreme stress. It's also possible for this to occur after prolonged exposure to stress.

Stress makes some people more susceptible to developing more serious or long-lasting physical health issues.

How Does Stress Affect Teens?

Teenagers, like adults, may be subjected to stress daily, making it important for them to develop coping mechanisms. Stress levels in adolescents tend to rise when they believe they are helpless in the face of a potentially harmful, challenging, or painful event. The following are examples of potential sources of stress for adolescents:

- Academic pressures and stresses

- Changes in their bodies

- Negative self-perceptions

- Peer or social issues at school

- Dangerous neighborhood or living conditions

- The conflict between parents leads to separation or divorce

- Illness that lasts a long time or significant family issues

- Tragic loss

- Changing your schooling situation

- Attempting to juggle too many tasks or having unrealistic goals

- Adverse effects on family finances

Some adolescents experience a crisis of stress. Anxiety, isolation, anger, physical sickness, and ineffective coping mechanisms like substance abuse are all possible outcomes.

Our brains and bodies react when we experience something emotionally taxing or physically uncomfortable. For example, as part of the " fight, flight, or freeze" response, one may experience an increase in heart rate and breathing rate, an increase in blood flow to the muscles of the arms and legs, and a decrease in body temperature (resulting in clammy hands and feet) , an upset stomach, or an overwhelming feeling of fear.

How is Stress Managed?

The stress response can be inhibited via the same mechanism that activates it. Once we determine that we are no longer in danger, our bodies and minds can undergo a series of adjustments that allow us to accomplish just that. Heart and breathing rates slow down, and one has an overall sense of well-being during this " relaxation response." Teens who learn to manage their stress using techniques like the " relaxation response" and other methods report feeling better in control of their reactions to stressful situations.

The following are methods by which parents can aid their teenagers:

Keep an eye on how adolescents behave, think, and feel to see whether stress is a factor.

- Pay attention to what teenagers are saying and watch for signs of overload.

- Cultivate and demonstrate abilities for dealing with stress.

- Encourage participation in sports and other community-building endeavors.

The following actions and strategies can help adolescents manage their stress levels:

- Maintain a regular eating and exercise schedule.

- Get a decent night' s rest and stick to a regular schedule.

- Caffeine can amplify negative emotions, so cutting back may help.

- Try to stay away from things like alcohol, tobacco, and narcotics that are unlawful.

- Discover the benefits of relaxation techniques (abdominal breathing and muscle relaxation techniques) .

- Build your confidence and learn to speak up for yourself. For instance, instead of being passive or aggressive, try saying something like, " I feel furious when you yell at me," or " Please stop yelling."

- Think about stressful circumstances you' ve been through and act them out. If public speaking makes you nervous, one solution is to enroll in a speech class.

- Gain some real-world experience in dealing with stress. Then, try breaking it down into smaller, more manageable chunks to accomplish something daunting.

- Reduce negative self-talk by replacing it with positive, neutral, or alternate thoughts. Change " my life will never get better" to " I may feel hopeless now, but my life will probably become better if I work at it and get some support."

- Instead of expecting perfection from yourself and others, learn to take pride in a well-done job.

- Get away from the tension for a while. Stress can be alleviated by listening to music, chatting with a friend, drawing, writing, or even spending time with a pet.

- Create a support system of good people who can encourage you when times get tough.

Teenagers can learn to cope with stress by adopting these and other methods. In addition, consultation with a child and adolescent psychiatrist or other certified mental health expert may be useful if a teen reports feeling stressed.

3.4 IMPROVING COMMUNICATION SKILLS

Converting one' s thoughts and feelings to another is crucial in any relationship. Teens can be actively engaged in learning, practicing, and developing their communication skills through experiential activities.

Everyone understands the importance of communication in both personal and professional relationships. However, teenagers are at the beginning stages of developing this ability. A more confident, self-assured, and self-aware adult can result from a teen's early training in effective and appropriate communication.

What are the signs of having Issues with Communication Skills?

We are more likely to shut down contact lines when we are preoccupied with ourselves. To name a few of the most notable:

Interrupting

That's something that everyone does. But, also, it's frustrating when other people do it to us. It isn't nice because it implies that what we say is more important than what the other person says.

Avoiding direct eye contact

Avoidance, preoccupation, anxiety or anxiousness, lack of interest, dishonesty, or insecurity are all signs of a lack of eye contact in Western culture. However, there are societies where it is considered rude to make direct eye contact, especially with an older person.

Negative or disinterested body language

What is more important, a person's words, how she expresses those words, or her actions while speaking or listening (nonverbal) ? According to studies, when your message is muddled, people tend to focus on what you aren't saying more than what you are. Emotions can be read through the body's expressions. It communicates to the other person whether they should continue the conversation with you or not.

Compelling alternatives

To what extent does the individual seeking to speak with you rank above other priorities? That is what their mind is wandering to if you're not paying attention. Get off the phone, switch off the TV, and close the book. Exhibit your care if you truly value this person.

Disturbed by strong feelings

You shouldn't be afraid to show your feelings when talking to people. God gave you feelings as part of who you are. However, your message may not get across if you let your emotions get the best of you when attempting to communicate. To the other person, all that matters is that you are upset, angry, or hurt. Think of the listener as well, as they are an important factor in any communication. How accepting of expressions of emotion are they likely to be? Do they withdraw when tensions rise? Whenever you feel like breaking down and crying or losing your cool? If that' s the case, it could be best to wait until your feelings have calmed before making a crucial point known.

Too preoccupied with one' s own needs

When you' re preoccupied with your wants and demands, it' s difficult to empathize with others. Take into consideration the people you know who are excellent speakers. Which is more important, their capacity to express themselves clearly or their openness to your perspective?

Anticipating that you can read people' s minds

We can assume that he is aware because he is the expert; this is a common complaint I hear from the ladies. My response is consistent regardless of the context. How can he know until you tell him? It' s unreasonable to expect another person to read your mind and understand your feelings. How long someone has known you is irrelevant. It makes no difference how many times you' ve talked. No matter how intuitive someone is, they cannot read your mind. They could know what' s going on or be completely clueless. However, they won' t know for sure unless you tell them.

Obtaining Approval

Sometimes the way we talk betrays an unhealthy form of submission or helplessness; this is often the case when one person is seen as the dominant one in a relationship. It could be a relative, a spouse, or a superior at work.

These are the kinds of queries that guarantee a negative response. Stop seeking approval before saying or doing what you know is right if expressing your convictions is vital to you. Even so, the other party may still choose to refuse your request. However, it is really important how you express your wants and needs.

Instead of just saying, " I want to do this," try expressing why it' s so important to you, how you and others would benefit, and how you plan to go about really doing it. Be ready to address any concerns raised by bringing some suggested solutions.

Punitive language

No amount of name-calling, snide accusations, or profanity is acceptable in healthy conversation. It would help if you didn' t speak in that manner and should make it clear that it' s not acceptable for the other person to speak to you in that manner, either.

How do Issues with Communication Skills Affect Teens?

How today' s adolescents interact significantly impacts the depth of their friendships and other social connections. Therefore, as parents and teachers, you and I need to observe how our teenagers interact socially and in the classroom to choose the best way to assist them in developing their communication skills.

Everyone knows that today' s youth struggle to speak for themselves and address their needs. They aren' t confident in their abilities. Thus they don' t speak up for themselves. Other kids will pick up on their insecurities early on, and they might be targeted for additional bullying.

Teens with social difficulties are vulnerable to being bullied. In addition, some of their friendships may be strained because they put up with terrible behavior from their pals and don' t know how to improve the dynamic. If your adolescent is experiencing such difficulties, you may be taking what is known as a passive approach.

Adolescents have an aggressive personality if they regularly display hostile behavior toward adults and other teens. In most cases, they show little concern for the other person' s welfare and may even resort to physically or verbally threatening behavior. Instead, they are focused solely on fulfilling their own needs.

They have trouble working in teams and are rude and aggressive to those they interact with. To get what they want, they could resort to intimidation or name-calling. Most of these young adults are responsible for creating an intimidating environment in school. The trouble arises, however, when they try to employ this tactic with a teacher or other authority figure.

Teens with an assertive approach know how to acquire what they want while considering the needs of those around them. They tend to use words in a way that is respectful and focused on finding a solution. They are gifted in both communication and problem-solving.

How are Communication Issues managed?

What matters most is that you keep talking to one another. Some ideas are:

- Remember that you only have one mouth and two ears, and use them for listening rather than talking; this is a gentle reminder that we need to listen more than talk – This is especially crucial when communicating with adolescents, as they may be more forthcoming if given a chance to speak in silence.

- If you want to keep in touch with your adolescent, it's important to set time for them at mealtimes like breakfast and dinner, even if they're preoccupied with schoolwork, friends, and other activities. Take them where they need to go or pick them up; this will open up new avenues of communication.

- Teenagers have a desire for solitude and should be given it. Be sure to ask permission before entering someone's room.

- Accompany them to their sports practices, watch the shows they like on TV, and listen to the music they like. Maintain an interest in what's going on in their life.

- Adolescence is when a child's identity rapidly evolves, and they need their parents' unconditional love more than ever. So they must hear it frequently. Show your affection by engaging in any form of physical contact they choose. Recognize their efforts, accept their shortcomings, be attentive when they have a problem, and take an active interest in how they intend to address it.

- Aid them as they attempt to find solutions to issues. Every young person needs to feel like they belong and are valued to develop a healthy sense of self-worth.

- (Spend some time relaxing and laughing with friends.) Positive emotions are a key component in establishing trusting relationships.

3.5 Improving Self-Esteem

How a person values and appreciates himself is what we mean when we talk about self-esteem. Teens face everyday challenges to their self-esteem from various sources, including family, peers, and the mirror. In addition, traumatic experiences can severely damage a teenager's self-esteem during these crucial years.

Some young people have such severe problems with their sense of self-worth that they can't break out of the prison of their low self-esteem and resort to harmful coping mechanisms. Some people join the wrong crowd or engage in self-destructive patterns because they believe doing so will help them gain the acceptance and popularity they want. They mistakenly think that if other people like them, they will feel good about themselves. People often get lost attempting to pinpoint the root cause or are mired in self-blame, convinced that they aren't bad enough to need assistance.

The benefits of encouraging a kid to value themselves can last a lifetime. Young people with a healthy sense of self-worth are less prone to engage in risky activities like substance misuse.

What are the Signs of Having Self-Esteem Issues?

In adolescence, there's a huge pressure to fit in and find your place among various groups. We all want to be seen and accepted by others, but self-esteem doesn't come from external approval. There are lots of ways to mask or ineffectively deal with low self-esteem.

Many people put up a front, pretending like things are great. They smile and laugh at school but go home to isolate themselves in their room, sleeping a lot and bottling up their emotions. Sometimes people become arrogant or bullies, putting others down in unproductive attempts to build themselves up.

How Do Self-Esteem Issues Affect Teens?

Many people working on bettering themselves worry that boosting their self-esteem would lead to inflated egos and a preoccupation with themselves. Arrogant and selfish people often give the impression that they have a high opinion of themselves. However, underneath this egocentric attitude lies a lack of confidence. Arrogant people try to boost their self-esteem by acting in self-centered or superior ways, but this rarely works. It's not very effective.

Bullies and arrogant people may feel temporarily boosted by the attention or laughter they receive when they humiliate others. Still, they are suffering from a deep-seated sense of inadequacy and unworthiness. In addition, hurting others to feel better about themselves is a fruitless endeavor that reinforces the person's self-doubt.

Many adolescents experience feelings that aren' t typical of their age group and may be symptomatic of a mood disorder or extremely low self-esteem. They are on their own to deal with emotions like anxiety, depression, or bewilderment about who they are without outside assistance. You are more likely to resort to harmful coping techniques when you lack support and appropriate direction.

How are Self-Esteem Issues Managed?

There is a common thread among people who suffer from low self-esteem, even though the causes of their insecurities and feelings of unworthiness can vary widely: they worry that they are inadequate and are inherently flawed. This apprehension can prevent you from moving forward with your plans. But it' s not insurmountable, and there are ways to boost your confidence and live a happier life.

It is natural to question whether or not this book will benefit you. Even positive changes might cause anxiety. Developing a healthy sense of self-worth requires you to take on new routines and abandon old ones. We anticipate that you may experience some resistance or apprehension as you adjust to this new way of being.

Keep in mind that everyone will have a different time of it when it comes to boosting their confidence. A key component of self-care is being patient and kind to oneself on the path to growth and self-acceptance. Exploring issues related to low self-esteem can be like opening a can of worms, leading us to dig up and deal with old hurts. Sometimes it seems like things are getting worse before they are. But take things slowly and have faith that a healthy sense of self-worth will emerge as you continue to put these strategies to use.

PART 2: PLAY THERAPY

CHAPTER 1: DEFINITION OF PLAY THERAPY

The establishment of play therapy in the 1940s, one of the most effective therapeutic tools for children, was a direct result of adults' realization and appreciation of this fact. According to the Association for Play Therapy (APT), "play therapy is the systematic use of a theoretical model to establish an interpersonal process where trained play therapists use the therapeutic powers of play to help clients prevent or resolve psychosocial difficulties and achieve optimal growth and development."

Play therapy allows teens to express and process their emotions about a given circumstance. It can also equip them with the cognitive and affective frameworks necessary for healthy growth. It's a must-have for effective communication, sound judgment, and emotional control.

Many adolescents are more amenable to attending appointments when informed that we will engage in activities rather than asking them numerous questions. I frequently tell my clients and their parents that I completely understand — if I sat in school all day, was asked questions all day, and (maybe) answered questions all day, I wouldn't want to do the same thing at night or on the weekend. By providing something entertaining and relaxing, you may break the monotony of the day and create opportunities for natural conversation, which occurs when you are relaxed, at ease, and enjoying the present.

If you ask your adolescent, "How was your day?" or "What's bothering you?" they will typically respond with a shrug or "I don't know." However, teens can access the emotional part of their brains through activities, games, and art, resulting in more effective, long-lasting growth. In addition, being in a context that permits indirect exploration of what's hurting them and how their day went is an opportunity kids may not have in other settings to manage their thoughts and emotions, which can be difficult to do with words alone.

Chapter 2: The Theory behind Play Therapy

When teenagers play, they can express themselves, regulate their emotions, gain new understanding, find joy, and solve issues. They talk about their deepest concerns, express their worries, and make sense of the world through play.

Therapists may identify with a certain theoretical framework to decide how best to satisfy a client's needs. There are numerous theoretical frameworks for play therapy, but the two most common are non-directive and directive. Since not all forms of play are created equal, these theoretical frameworks help therapists select the type of play most beneficial to their patients.

Non-Directive Play Therapy

Virginia Axline established the concept of non-directive play therapy in the 1940s. It is based on the idea that children will utilize their natural medium of play to best express an issue they have with the therapist. This approach was popularized in the 2010 book " Child-Centered Play Therapy." The therapist in non-directive play therapy steps back and lets the kid direct the activity.

Similar to a play-by-play announcer during a sporting event, a therapist in a non-directive therapy relationship will verbally track the client's actions. The therapist will provide support, emphasize symptom-related themes, and provide growth opportunities while the client's progress is tracked.

Directive Play Therapy

Therapy, in which the therapist actively guides the client through activity, is called " directive play therapy." The therapist employs a more comprehensive therapeutic tool in a playful context, like relaxation techniques or problem resolution. Art, movement, music, games, toys, role-play, snacks, and sometimes even parents or caregivers can be incorporated into therapy sessions to help clients develop a particular skill, target a specific moment in time, and prepare a client to begin processing a traumatic event, assess a specific issue, identify feelings, learn emotional regulation tools, or build understanding.

Play therapists often incorporate directed tasks into otherwise unstructured sessions, actively involving their clients while keeping close tabs on their progress through verbal tracking.

CHAPTER 3: PLAY THERAPY AND TEENS

Involving your teen in activities like these can help them in many ways.

- The first step in modifying your child's behavior is to fortify the bond between you and your youngster.

- To help your child recognize and cope with their feelings, you first need to help them gain insight into their mental state.

- Help your kid accept and understand their feelings without letting them control them by teaching them how to manage their emotions better.

- Assist your youngster in rediscovering the joys of play. Quite a few of the families I help have mentioned that their kids can't get enough screen time. This situation may result in various behavioral issues, including changes in impulse control and sleep habits, increased tantrums, aggressive behaviors, and whining. The exercises in this book can help parents wean their children off their electronic devices.

- Teens who have trouble maintaining healthy sleep patterns should see an improvement in their sleep patterns.

- Encourage open lines of communication between mom, dad, and the kids.

- Improving your child's social skills is a must.

- Develop more patience and the ability to think before acting.

- Assist a child who is experiencing anxiety in handling their concerns.

- Encourage your youngster to learn the fundamentals of mindfulness and stress reduction.

Chapter 4: General Play Therapy Activities

Feelings Drawing

Feelings like anger, sadness, worry, and guilt are natural human experiences. Just because you're emotionally stable doesn't mean you never feel sad or angry; it just means you're aware of your feelings and can choose how to react to them. You can use this game as a playful and expressive way to assist your teen in learning to recognize and accept their emotions.

MATERIALS: Drawing materials (paper, crayons, markers, paints, or colored pencils)

First, you should tell your kid that everyone has emotions. One technique to get a sense of our emotional state is to tune inside and take stock of our thoughts and bodily sensations.

Assist them in doing a quick self-check by asking questions like how they feel or what they think about.

Give them a piece of paper and some pencils and have them tell you how they feel. Then, let them color and draw what they see on the interior with as few guidelines as possible.

The next time you play with your kid, remind them to take stock of how they're feeling; this is fun to do after you get home from school. Teens develop a more intuitive awareness of their emotions when they take the time to check in with how they're regularly feeling.

Feelings Playlist

Many people find that when they make music, they are expressing themselves in a way that comes easily to them. I have found this exercise particularly useful for somewhat older children in helping them open up about their feelings in a non-threatening environment.

1. Tell your kid you will share unique stories about how you felt during the day.

2. Please encourage your child to express their emotions throughout the day, not with words but with music, by having them compile a playlist. (You can use any web-based music service, such as Spotify, Apple Music, or YouTube.)

3. Pick songs that express your feelings throughout the day and add them to your child's playlist.

4. Take turns playing each other's music.

Playing Tip: Express aloud what the song does to your emotions. For example, listening to a pleasant, lively tune can reflect on the joyful sensation it provides. On the other hand, listening to a feisty tune may inspire some aggressive movement.

Hug Challenge

The phrase "sensory input" explains how the human body processes our senses. Depending on the sensation, this information can either relax and comfort your teen or upset and overwhelm them. All of it will come down to the individual's sensory requirements.

For example, through this exercise, they will become aware of the contrasting effects of various forms of physical contact, such as a bear hug and a high-five. You can refer to this information when you feel your child could use some extra help relaxing.

MATERIALS: Blanket

1. Tell your kid you're going to undertake a hug experiment.

2. Describe a hug using the chart below. After describing this form of a hug, please encourage your child to pay attention to how it makes them feel.

3. Help your youngster fill out the chart by transcribing their answers if necessary.

Let your teen take charge of this "hug adventure." Give each other a variety of embraces and discuss the sensations they elicit in your bodies.

Place an X in the box to best describe how this hug makes you feel		Calm, happy, loved	Agitated, annoyed, or angry
Bear Hug	Wrap your arms around your teen and give them a tight squeeze.	- -	- -
Butterfly Hug	Cross your arms across your chest, placing your right hand on your left and your left hand on your right bicep. Gently tap your hands against your bicep back and forth, just like a butterfly flapping its wings. You can have your child give themselves a butterfly hug, or you can have them sit in your lap as you hug them. Allow your child to choose!	- -	- -
Hand Hug	Place your right palm into your teen's left palm as if you were to give each other a high five. Next, gently wrap your thumbs around the back of each other's hands.	- -	- -
Burrito Hug	Roll your teen up in a big blanket as if you were going to make them into a big, teen-sized burrito. Then, please give them a big bear hug while they're in their burrito.	- -	- -

Sensational Walk

Getting the family out for fresh air and exercise is as simple as going for a stroll. Your teen's participation, connection, understanding of the outdoors, and five senses can benefit from this fun addition.

1. Plan a walk outside with your kid and the rest of the family – This is an excellent activity for the time between the end of the school day and the beginning of your teen's homework.

2. Playfully encourage your teen to pay attention to the world by asking them questions about what they see, hear, smell, taste, and feel while you stroll together. Please encourage them to take stock of their visual faculties by asking them to list five objects they can currently make out.

3. Encourage your kid to take note of their sense of smell by having them smell different items. Indulge your sense of smell by taking a moment to appreciate the aroma of various plants and flowers.

4. Encourage your teen's tactile sense by drawing their attention to the sensations experienced by their feet when they walk on different surfaces, such as grass and pavement.

5. Take a moment to focus on your teen's auditory sense. Can they hear anything like birds, the wind, or cars?

6. While walking together with your teen, have them observe how their senses change.

7. If you'd like, after you get back from your stroll, have your kid fill out the activities below (if you're using them) to help them remember and reflect on what they saw.

Help your teen connect with their senses by pointing out what you're noticing with your senses as you play with them.

Draw a picture of something you saw	Draw a picture of something you felt
Draw a picture of something you smelled	Draw a picture of something you heard

Mind Jar

With your teen, you will make a tool that may be used for deep breathing, calming, and concentrating on the present moment.

MATERIALS: Mason jar, craft glitter (various colors) , glitter glue, water

1. You and your teen should fill the jar with water halfway.

2. Let your kids use as much glitter as they like. Authorize the blending of colors and the exercise of imagination!

3. Use around a medium-sized squeeze of glitter glue. While there is no perfect science to this, using too much glitter glue will not yield the desired results. To begin, give the bottle three good squeezes.

4. Put the lid on the jar and fill it with water to the top.

5. Begin vigorously shaking the container to combine the glitter and glue with the water.

6. Shake the Mind Jar once more, set it on the counter, and observe as its vibrant contents gradually rest in a condition of serenity and peace. As the jar settles, remind your youngster to take a deep breath.

7. Explain that the Mind Jar might stand for:

The contents become chaotic, messy, and fast-moving when the jar is shaken. When we feel very confused, it' s like this on the inside of our heads and bodies. However, the jar can regain its sense of tranquility when we give it some breathing room and deep breaths.

If your youngster is agitated and could benefit from some distance, time, and deep breathing, this jar can serve as a timer.

Use the jar as a prop in a game of observation. Start by shaking the jar, then take turns pointing out different features as the glitter settles. To illustrate this point, consider the glitter and how its various sizes and colors cause it to settle at varying rates.

CHAPTER 5: PLAY THERAPY FOR SPECIFIC ISSUES

5.1 ANXIETY

MY TOP FIVE WORRIES

Examining and assessing one's fears is a key step in learning about anxiety.

What You'll Need: Pencils and paper

Duration: 15 to 20 minutes

Best for: 1 to 6 people

LEADING THE ACTIVITY

1. Explain how stress and worry can impair day-to-day functioning. Get the teen or teens to think of all the ways anxiety affects them.

2. Explain how focusing on one's anxieties can allow one to pinpoint the origins of their distress.

3. Have them write down any concerns that come to mind after thinking about them for 2 minutes.

4. After going over this list, they should select their "Top 5" concerns and write them down on a new sheet of paper, along with any further comments they may have about each.

5. Discuss their top five concerns with the group.

DISCUSSION QUESTIONS

- What are some of your biggest worries?

- What concerns do you all have in common?

- In what ways might learning about your concerns serve as a starting point for calming your nerves?

PRO TIPS

- Encourage imagination by prodding participants with questions and statements during the brainstorming session. As an illustration, consider the question, " What is your biggest concern about school?"

- If you have access to a dry-erase board, feel free to jot down your concerns.

- Make it clear that their concerns are all warranted.

ANXIETY BOARD GAME

Making a board game about anxiety and how it affects people is a great way to open up a conversation about these issues.

What You' ll Need: Poster board; markers; pencils; dice; simple objects to use as game pieces

Duration: 20 to 40 minutes

Best for: 2 to 10 people

LEADING THE ACTIVITY

First, break the teenagers into smaller groups. Challenge them to design a board game that explores healthy and unhealthy approaches to managing anxiety. The game' s path is recommended to be between 15 and 20 squares long.

- One-half of the squares should have upbeat numbers (between one and three) and include constructive self-talk or coping mechanisms.

- The other half should be negative (1–3) and include a negative coping strategy.

After each team has completed a board, they should trade with another and begin playing according to the regulations below:

- Each player takes it in turn, choosing a piece, then rolling the dice to advance it to the next available square.

- The player examines the text on the square and why it will lead to advancement or setback.

- The adolescent then advances the calculated distance.
- Each player races to the finish line to determine who can win first.

DISCUSSION QUESTIONS

- How did it feel to design your board game? What did you learn about anxiety as a result of this?
- Is there anything unique you saw on your friends' game boards?

PRO TIPS

- Make the game more interesting by adding new types of squares, such as "lose a round" or "double the dice roll." Be certain that appropriate anxiety reactions are added to these grids.
- Split the time spent on this into two parts: making the game and playing it.

Mountain Meditation

A Guided Meditation Approach to Overcoming Anxious Thoughts

What You'll Need: No materials are needed

Duration: 15 to 20 minutes

Best for: 1 to 5 people

LEADING THE ACTIVITY

1. Discuss how anxiety simply passes through us like other thoughts or emotions. While it may be uncomfortable at the moment, it eventually subsides.
2. With teen(s) seated or standing in a comfortable position and their eyes closed, guide them through the following meditation:

- You are a mountain: tall, strong, and grounded.

- It's springtime. With spring comes storms. The storms are strong but eventually pass, just like your anxious thoughts.

- Now comes summer. The heat feels uncomfortable, but your inner core remains cool and collected.

- Autumn brings changes. The leaves on your trees turn beautiful colors. You may be anxious about these changes, but you stand tall.

- Winter brings cold and darkness. But even during the coldest nights, you stand strong. You know it will pass.

- As seasons pass, things change all around you, but your strength keeps you grounded, capable of managing whatever comes your way. You are a mountain. You are strong.

- Allow teens to take a few deep breaths and reorient to the room.

DISCUSSION QUESTIONS

- Did you find this exercise provided a new way of thinking about your anxiety? How?

- How can you stay resilient when things are tough by remembering that your anxiety is only fleeting?

PRO TIPS

- During this time, please do your best to focus without interruption.

- In between each prompt, give yourself time to ponder deeply.

ANXIETY COPING PLAN

What You'll Need: Pencils and paper

Duration: 20 to 25 minutes

Best for: 1 to 4 people

LEADING THE ACTIVITY

1. Explain how a set strategy might help you make sound decisions when feeling nervous.

2. Clarify that effective methods of managing anxiety are important to any viable coping strategy.

3. Have the adolescent or adolescent group write at the top of a sheet of paper at least five persons, places, or things that cause them to worry.

4. Have the adolescent write down at least three broad coping strategies they've found to control anxiety below the list of things that tend to set off their anxiety.

5. Have the teens plan how they'll handle the situation on the back. Encourage them to write at least five introductory " I" statements in which they identify their worry and outline their strategy for overcoming it. For example, " I often talk to my best friend on the phone to alleviate my feelings of isolation and anxiety."

6. Share your thoughts and observations as you go along.

DISCUSSION QUESTIONS

- Tell me about a moment when you were nervous and unsure what to do.

- When dealing with anxiety, why is it helpful to have a set of techniques at your disposal?

- Is there a specific way in which the development of this coping strategy has allowed you to understand better and manage your anxiety?

PRO TIPS

- Since this is a highly customized experience, keeping the group size small is best—adolescents who have already engaged in activities designed to reduce anxiety benefit greatly from this intervention.

- Teens should offer concrete, plausible coping mechanisms for each " I" assertion.

- Make sure there's a reward system in place for when the teen meets their part of the bargain. " I can reward myself when I employ the coping mechanisms I described."

5.2 Depression

We are Connected

Improve Your Mood by Strengthening Your Social Connections

What You'll Need: Ball

Duration: 15 to 20 minutes

Best for: 4 to 10 people

LEADING THE ACTIVITY

1. Talk about how the more people we know, the more we realize how much we have in common with them. Having social media connections can help you feel less alone.

2. Have everyone form a circle, keeping at least a two-shoulder-width distance between each other.

3. Pass the ball to an adolescent and have them describe their favorite activity; for example, "I like tennis."

4. Toss the ball to another teen and have them take a shot.

5. Have them catch the ball and respond to the first sentence. For example, "I like tennis too, but I prefer baseball,"

6. Keep going for as long as you can!

DISCUSSION QUESTIONS

- How much do you know about the other members of the group now?

- Explain one link you established here.

- To what extent it may help you cope with depression if you found out you had more in common with your peers?

PRO TIPS

- If a youngster can' t think of anything to agree with the previous remark, they can always just agree with it and add their twist. For instance, " I' ve always been more interested in spending time outside than art."

- Teens should be prompted to provide more details than previously stated. For instance, " I, too, enjoy the pastime of playing video games. My preference in video games would have to be."

- You can extend the game by discussing anything other than the rules, such as your favorite meals or earliest memories.

GET MOVING… FEEL BETTER

Working out can help alleviate depression.

What You' ll Need: Open area

Duration: 15 to 20 minutes

Best for: 3 to 8 people

LEADING THE ACTIVITY

1. Explain how physical activity alleviates depression, including the release of endorphins and other feel-good brain chemicals and the resulting boost in self-esteem.

2. To begin, have everyone stand at least four shoulder-width away from each other.

3. Explain that they will engage in a brief, low-impact workout.

4. Instruct them to proceed as follows:

- Repeat this for 30 seconds while maintaining a brisk walking pace.

- Stand up straight and raise your arms overhead. Breathe deeply for five seconds.

- Exercise by performing 30 seconds of jumping jacks.

- Put your hands on your head, stand straight up, and lean to the right. To hold, wait 25 seconds. Turn it over and do the same thing.

- March in place for 30 seconds.

- Stand for 45 seconds with your weight on your left foot. Then switch to your Right foot.

- Get your heart rate up by jogging in place for 30 seconds.

- If you want to feel your entire body relax, stand tall, breathe deeply five times, and then feel free to sit back down.

5. Demonstrate how the mood-enhancing benefits of exercise and yoga are incorporated into this program.

DISCUSSION QUESTIONS

- What was your favorite physical activity, and why?

- How did you feel after doing the routine?

- How can working out for even a little time each day help you feel better?

PRO TIPS

- Exercises and duration should be modified according to the group' s skill level.

- Do not specify how long they should spend on each activity; doing so may deter them.

MY COMMUNITY, MY RESOURCES,

Identifying and mapping community-based depression support services

What You' ll Need: Paper; pencils; colored pencils; markers

Duration: 20 to 30 minutes

Best for: 1 to 5 people

LEADING THE ACTIVITY

1. Talk about times when you or your teen felt sad or isolated.

2. Consider possible supports that might be helpful as they deal with depression.

3. Allow the adolescent time to reflect on the persons or resources they can turn to when their depression overwhelms them. Prompt them with questions like, " Who can you talk to about your feelings?" if necessary.

4. Have them make a " roadmap" to locate reliable resources to aid depression management.

5. Have them mark as many secure landmarks as possible and explain why they are useful.

6. Talk about the maps with others.

DISCUSSION QUESTIONS

- Where do you turn for help when you' re feeling down? Why?

- Are there any familiar places you can visit when feeling down?

- How might knowing where to turn for assistance be encouraged by a list of local resources?

PRO TIPS

- Help the teen(s) locate points of interest by expanding on their first list of ideas.

- Permit them to assign a different shade to each of their landmarks. Places that make them joyful may be orange, while those who help them relax could be blue.

- If students have trouble drawing a map, they can try writing " If... then..." phrases instead. For example, consider the following: " I know I can always turn to my best buddy for advice and comfort if I feel overwhelmed by the circumstances in my family."

SELF-CARE BRAINSTORM

Methods of self-care for treating depression

What You' ll Need: Pencils and paper

Duration: 20 to 25 minutes

Best for: 1 to 4 people

LEADING THE ACTIVITY

1. Self-care is the proactive maintenance of one's physical, mental, and social well-being. Request that the teen or teens give specific instances. The act of self-care can take numerous forms. Therefore, it's important to stress that there are options.

2. Introduce the five dimensions of health: physiological, mental, social, intellectual, and spiritual. Get the adolescent (or teens) to define each group and provide some examples. Have them make six columns on a sheet of paper, one for each group.

3. Give them a minute or two to consider and write down ideas for self-care across all categories.

4. Number the ideas for self-care from 1 to 5 stars and have them circle the ones most helpful to them.

5. Allow them to discuss self-care strategies and share their own.

DISCUSSION QUESTIONS

- Share some of your preferred methods of self-care.

- Where did you have the most trouble thinking of ideas?

- What ways do you think self-care can aid depression management?

PRO TIPS

- Poster boards with different groups should be displayed in a large space. Then, have the teen or teens visit each station to contribute their suggestions.

- Before coming up with ideas, ensure they have a firm grasp of the available options.

- Discuss the results with them and discuss how good self-care can help alleviate depressive symptoms if that is an issue.

5.3 Stress

Good and Bad Stress

We resolve issues by understanding the sources of stress and differentiating beneficial from harmful stress.

What You'll Need: Pencils and paper; dry-erase board and markers

Duration: 15 to 20 minutes

Best for: 1 to 6 people

LEADING THE ACTIVITY

1. Explain what stress is and how it fits into your daily life, especially if you're a teenager.

2. Allow the adolescent some time to think about and list the things causing them stress.

3. Define positive or temporary stress like a new job that helps us focus and perform better.

4. Define negative stress or persistent sources of strain that are detrimental to health, well-being, and productivity, such as recurrent family problems.

5. Take a dry-erase board and make two columns, one for positive and negative stress.

6. Have the teen or teens write three stressors from their list on the board.

7. Talk about what you learned from this exercise.

DISCUSSION QUESTIONS

- When it comes to stress, how can you know if you're getting the good kind or the bad kind?

- What general strains did you encounter while participating in this exercise?

- How can you better manage stress if you don't know the difference between good and bad?

PRO TIPS

- If you want your teen to understand the difference between healthy and unhealthy stress, give them plenty of instances of both.

- Suppose you' re having trouble getting a teen to open up about the stresses in their lives. In that case, you may try collecting samples of these stressors anonymously and then having them sort them into categories.

- Stress affects people differently; thus, the right response varies from person to person.

HOW STRESS AFFECTS MY BODY

Examining how stress manifests in the body

What You' ll Need: Paper; colored pencils (green, yellow, and red)

Duration: 15 to 20 minutes

Best for: 1 to 8 people

LEADING THE ACTIVITY

1. Explain the numerous physiological effects of stress.

2. Have the adolescent(s) consider what stresses them out and pay attention (without judgment) to where they feel tension or tightness in their body (1 to 2 minutes) .

3. Give them some time to gather their bearings in the space again.

4. Have them sketch a diagram of their body and color in the parts stressed out by the scenario they' ve been thinking about. Get them to use green for no sensations, yellow for mild tightness or tension, and red for severe discomfort.

5. Allow them to talk to one another.

DISCUSSION QUESTIONS

- Where did you feel the effects of stress the most in your body? So, how did you feel?

- Where did stress manifest itself in people' s bodies the most often?

- Knowing how your body reacts to stress might be a useful indicator of how stressed you are.

PRO TIPS

- The best way to keep from being triggered during introspection is to keep stress at a moderate level. Indicate by some means what you mean.

- To whichever adolescent you may be speaking, please emphasize that there is no single, correct way to deal with stress.

- Teens who are grieving or have experienced significant trauma may not be able to participate in this activity without additional support.

PROCRASTINATION STRESS

Keep in mind the stress that procrastination can cause.

What You' ll Need: Simple puzzles, word games, or other challenging activities

Duration: 20 to 25 minutes

Best for: 1 to 8 people

LEADING THE ACTIVITY

1. Give each adolescent a puzzle or other exercise with an unrealistically low time constraint.

2. Instruct the teen(s) to get started and keep them apprised of progress as time passes. Such as, " There is only one minute left." (This is an example of the time constraints of putting things off.)

3. When the timer goes off, stop playing. Instead, probe your teen' s emotions by inquiring about their state of mind.

4. Have the adolescent seek out new games or other pursuits.

5. Start the clock over and give yourself enough time to finish.

6. " You' re doing great. Take your time and focus" are examples of the most encouraging prompts you should give.

7. Call time when the allotted time has elapsed or when all of the teens have finished the task.

8. Talk about how the teen or teens felt at this point. Discuss how reducing their workload and giving them more time to do things might help them relax.

DISCUSSION QUESTIONS

- What did you think as I ticked off the remaining time till you have to do the task?

- Was the task simpler to finish when you had more time and less pressure?

- How does putting things off cause stress?

PRO TIPS

- Select events that will both interest and challenge your teenagers. Games like mazes and " find the difference" exercises can also be effective.

- Maintain interest in the second half of the task by keeping tabs on how frustrated they are after completing the first.

- When working in bigger groups, having the teens pair up may be helpful.

PERFECTION STRESS

Knowing the link between perfectionism and stress encourages young people to accept their " flaws."

What You' ll Need: Dry-erase board and marker

Duration: 15 to 20 minutes

Best for: 2 to 8 people

LEADING THE ACTIVITY

1. Explain perfectionism and how it can lead to high pressure and anxiety levels.

2. Create a list of the unattainable standards teenagers must overcome in their quest for perfection. Then, please put them in writing and post them.

3. Locate the origins of these presumptions and record them on a separate piece of paper.

4. Plead for concrete instances of how each stressor manifests itself.

5. Explain how letting go of perfectionism and accepting one's flaws might help one live a happier, more fulfilled life.

6. Ask the adolescent to talk about a flaw they like about themselves.

7. To accept some flaws is not to give up. You must explain in point number seven. Rather, it's an occasion to appreciate individuality and be kinder to oneself.

DISCUSSION QUESTIONS

- Exactly which of these anticipations gives you the most anxiety right now?

- What causes you to feel inadequate?

- How could coming to terms with your flaws make it easier to handle stress?

PRO TIPS

- Give people a chance to explain why certain goals are unattainable.

- Teens should be encouraged to discuss how others' unrealistic expectations positively affect them without resorting to name-calling.

- Some seemingly impossible goals like doing great in school may be doable. Distinguish between high expectations and unreasonable ones.

EMOJI STRESS BALL

How to make stress balls and when to use them.

What You'll Need: Balloons; baking soda; hair conditioner; bowls; spoons; scissors; empty plastic water bottles; permanent or dry-erase markers

Duration: 15 to 20 minutes

Best for: 1 to 6 people

Prep: Make a stress ball ahead of time as an example of the finished project.

LEADING THE ACTIVITY

1. Explain how using a stress ball can help you calm down, refocus, and reduce the production of stress hormones.

2. Have the teen(s) make their stress balls like the one you just made:

- Put 2 cups of baking soda in a large bowl.

- Combine a half-cup of hair conditioner with the other ingredients.

- Recycled plastic water bottles can be used. However, the top third should be removed; this is the funnel that will be used.

- Connect the balloon' s aperture to the bottle' s.

- Fill the remaining bottle portion with the combined baking soda and hair conditioner.

- The spoonful of the mixture should be pushed inside the balloon.

- Please ensure there are no stray air bubbles in the balloon before closing it.

- Put an emoji face on it using some markers.

DISCUSSION QUESTIONS

- How did you express your stress with your stress ball in emoji? Why?

- How does giving a stress ball help reduce tension and refocus attention?

PRO TIPS

- The stress ball' s softness is proportional to the amount of hair conditioner utilized.

- Talk about how and when using a stress ball might help you.

5.4 IMPROVING COMMUNICATION SKILLS

ACTIVE LISTENING:

Learning more about other people through attentive listening.

What You' ll Need: No materials are needed

Duration: 15 to 20 minutes

Best for: 2 to 10 people

LEADING THE ACTIVITY

1. Explain that active listening is a method of hearing someone' s words to retain and recall them to grasp their meaning fully. Provide illustrative instances of how you use active listening techniques like making eye contact and paraphrasing.

2. Have the youths actively or poorly exhibit their listening abilities.

3. Have the teens form pairs and have one do the introducing while the other employs active listening. Teens should be given three minutes to introduce themselves.

4. Once the three minutes are up, have the students who have been actively listening introduce their partners to the class.

5. Have them swap places and do it again.

6. Talk about how you both benefited from your partner' s active listening skills.

DISCUSSION QUESTIONS

- What did you find difficult about using active listening skills? Easy?

- How did it make you feel when your conversational partner actively listened to you as you introduced yourself?

- In what ways can you improve your communication skills through active listening?

PRO TIPS

- Put teenagers together with people they don' t know well, if feasible.

- Give the teens a list of subjects they can discuss to open up more.

- Describe several excellent instances of attentive listening that you witnessed after completing the task.

GUESS MY EMOTION

The use of nonverbal behavior as an expression of emotion

What You' ll Need: No materials are needed

Duration: 15 to 20 minutes

Best for: 2 to 10 people

LEADING THE ACTIVITY

1. Explain the meaning of nonverbal communication and stress its significance alongside spoken exchanges.

2. Explain the significance of nonverbal cues, such as the use of clenched fists to convey anger or crossed arms to indicate that one isn' t paying attention.

3. Have one adolescent perform an emotional expression silently. Then, to get people to guess your feelings, you can play a guessing game.

4. Have each adolescent perform a few scenes in which they express a wide range of feelings.

5. Explain how being aware of and recognizing nonverbal communication might help young people be more empathic and " tuned in" during conversations.

DISCUSSION QUESTIONS

- Give an example of a moment when you read someone' s emotions without them having to say anything. Say what you saw.

- Can you think of an instance where your body language conveyed conflicting messages?

- How may paying attention to nonverbal cues help you connect with others more effectively?

PRO TIPS
- Give the teenagers an emotion to act out from a predetermined list rather than letting them pick their own.
- Tell the teens to form groups of two and act out different feelings.
- When an adolescent correctly identifies an emotion, inquire about the telltale signs.

KEEP THE CANDY!

Communicating effectively and confidently to reach your objectives

What You' ll Need: Candy or any other desirable items (about five pieces for each teen)

Duration: 15 to 20 minutes

Best for: 2 to 8 people

LEADING THE ACTIVITY
1. Explain the " three c' s" (confidence, clarity, and control) and provide some examples of how they might be used in assertive communication.
2. Have the teens come up with and then explore various examples of assertive communication: Just how forceful (or passive/ aggressive) are they?
3. Give a handful of chocolates to a single teenager. Allow the other teens a minute or two to convince the one holding the candy to part with it. Then, use strong language to convince the kid holding the sweets that they should retain them.
4. After the allotted time, have the teens write a summary of their stay there.
5. Let the other kids take turns holding the candy and using their aggressive communication skills to keep it.
6. Talk about the various forms of interaction throughout the exercise.

DISCUSSION QUESTIONS

- What was going through your head as someone tried to take the sweets from you? Describe an instance in which you exhibited aggressive behavior.

- Give an example of when it would have been preferable to use assertive language rather than aggressive or passive language.

- What are the benefits of learning to communicate assertively?

PRO TIPS

- Do a quick " time-out and check-in" session to reorient the group if a teen is getting irritated or aggressive during the activity.

- After each one to two-minute segment, emphasize a single excellent phrase or conduct that exemplifies forceful communication.

APOLOGIZING SINCERELY

Motivating young people to provide sincere apologies.

What You' ll Need: Plastic Easter eggs filled with coins (or another object for teens to toss to each other)

Duration: 10 to 15 minutes

Best for: 4 to 14 people

LEADING THE ACTIVITY

1. Have a conversation about what is and is not acceptable behavior while apologizing. Emphasize positive examples, such as honesty and not blaming others.

2. Have the teens form two lines, about three feet apart, with the youths in each line facing each other.

3. Distribute the eggs. Then, have the groups throw their eggs back and forth. Every time a teen catches an egg, they go backward.

4. Have the person who missed or dropped the egg apologize profusely.

5. If you believe their apologies were sincere, let play resume.

6. Make them both apologize if it's a teenage couple, and you can't tell which one started it.

7. If you suspect an apology is not genuine, suggest that the parties take time apart to discuss it.

8. Call time on the game if there is only one remaining pair or if the pairings are more than 10 feet apart.

9. Have the youths who were people kicked out of the game talk about why their apologies weren't real and how they may be made better.

DISCUSSION QUESTIONS

- Give an account of how you felt when you had to apologize to a comrade in the heat of battle.

- What characteristics did the apologizer possess that convinced you they truly meant what they said?

- The ability to apologize is crucial in interpersonal interactions; how is this so?

PRO TIPS

- You can cap the number of apologies a pair can make to keep playing instead of letting them continue after each.

- If you're playing in a confined space, make each throw more difficult. To illustrate, have the two teenagers each stand on one foot.

5.5 Improving Self-Esteem

Finding Faith in Yourself

To boost your self-esteem, you need to have faith in yourself. Even if you placed yourself at the very bottom of the self-esteem continuum, the good news is that you already have a small seed of hope that improving your self-esteem is achievable and valuable just by reading this book. So, use that to propel you forward while we investigate your uncertainty.

Faith in Yourself Quiz

Answer " true" or " false" to the following questions:

I trust myself to . . .

1.	Make good decisions.	**True**	**False**
2.	Share my opinions and ideas.	**True**	**False**
3.	Speak up for me.	**True**	**False**
4.	Take healthy risks.	**True**	**False**
5.	Say " no" to things that can harm me.	**True**	**False**
6.	Care for my well-being.	**True**	**False**
7.	Engage in healthy relationships.	**True**	**False**
8.	Walk away from unhealthy relationships.	**True**	**False**
9.	Take credit for my accomplishments.	**True**	**False**

10.	Ask for help when needed.	**True**	**False**
11.	Avoid procrastination.	**True**	**False**
12.	Set realistic goals.	**True**	**False**
13.	Put new tools I learn into practice.	**True**	**False**
14.	Stay motivated to build self-esteem.	**True**	**False**

If you answered yes to the majority of the questions above, you should be commended. If you compare yourself to the average person, you may have an easier time boosting your confidence. It's very okay if most of your answers were false.

People with low self-esteem often struggle with decision-making, self-care, healthy relationships, and the motivation to make positive changes. This book will show you how to do those things and more.

RECRUITING A FRIEND

If you took our self-trust quiz and scored low, you may want to find a friend who also wants to boost their self-esteem and work through this book alongside you if you want to increase your chances of success. Achieving your goals may be as easy as saying them out loud.

Consider sharing your plans to improve your sense of self-worth with the following three people:

1. _____

2. _____

3. _____

Is there anything holding you back from sharing your plans to boost your self-esteem with others?

_____

_____

_____

Just tell one person what you want to accomplish and see what happens.

Noticing Negative Self-Talk

Self-awareness is one of the most powerful weapons against low self-esteem, sadness, and anxiety. The term " self-talk" describes the never-ending stream of thoughts, both consciously and unconsciously, that run through your head daily. Unfortunately, most of us have a habit of constantly criticizing ourselves or causing anxiety with our inner monologue. If we want to feel better, we must train ourselves to take charge of our internal dialogue and replace negative or discouraging thoughts with more positive ones.

Distorted and Irrational Thinking

The following are some of the most common erroneous messages and irrational beliefs that make up negative self-talk. Look at the descriptions and ask yourself if and when you ever engage in these unhelpful modes of thinking:

BLACK-AND-WHITE THINKING	MINIMIZATION
Black-and-white or all-or-nothing thinking is when you think in extreme ways. Things are either all good or all bad.	Minimization is when you downplay the importance of your strengths and accomplishments.
EXAMPLES:	EXAMPLES:
That test was hard. I am going to fail the class. She ignored my text. Everyone hates me. Nothing ever works out for me.	I' ve done well so far, but I might mess up and fail the class.

	I got a 90% on the test. I can't believe I didn't get a perfect score.
	They invited me to the party because they felt sorry for me.
I DO THIS WHEN:	I DO THIS WHEN:
CATASTROPHIZING	PERSONALIZATION
Catastrophizing is when you magnify the negatives. You dwell on mistakes and blow problems out of proportion.	Personalization is when you always assume responsibility for anything that goes wrong.
EXAMPLES:	EXAMPLES:
Since I made this mistake, I should probably just quit. He broke up with me. I'm probably never going to find happiness. I failed this exam and will never get into any colleges.	It's my fault my friends aren't talking to me. I always ruin everything. I'm just not smart enough.
I DO THIS WHEN:	I DO THIS WHEN:
MIND READING AND JUMPING TO CONCLUSIONS	LABELING

Mind reading and jumping to conclusions are assumptions that others negatively judge you without valid reasons, or you fixate on the worst-case scenario as your default.	Labeling is when you assign yourself negative labels or call yourself mean names.
EXAMPLES:	EXAMPLES:
I'm going to fail, and things are never going to work out. They don't like me. They just feel sorry for me. I can't be happy if she doesn't want to be with me.	I'm such an idiot. I'm an incompetent failure. I'm a freak.
I DO THIS WHEN:	I DO THIS WHEN:

This kind of negative thinking leads to a gloomy outlook, which undermines one's ability to feel good about oneself and keep a healthy sense of self-worth. Sometimes the remarks become self-fulfilling prophecies and set you up for failure. However, you can enhance your feelings by keeping track of your thoughts and attempting to alter your fundamental worldview.

Know Who You Are

The adolescent years are a time of self-discovery and growing confidence in one's uniqueness. Sometimes, however, you may take a detour that causes you to forget who you are. So, let's take a moment to reconnect with who you are.

All About Me

A low sense of self-worth might make it hard to recognize even the most fundamental preferences. You can allow other people's opinions to influence your own, or you might allow depression to prevent you from seeing the bright side of life. Recognizing one's preferences is an important step in fostering self-respect.

Please take a few minutes to respond to the following questionnaire:

My favorite color is_____

My favorite food is_____

My favorite place is _____

My favorite activity is_____

My favorite hobby or interest is_____

My favorite class or subject is_____

My least favorite thing to do is_____

My least favorite class or subject is_____

My favorite show, movie, or book is_____

My favorite music or song is_____

When I have alone time, I like to_____

If I could choose anywhere to go, it would be_____

As a child, when I grew up, I wanted to be_____

My dream job would be_____

If I could have dinner with anyone, I would choose_____

One of my favorite memories is_____

One of my greatest accomplishments is_____

One of my greatest challenges has been_____

A defining moment in my life so far has been_____

If any of the abovementioned issues proved challenging, consider what stood in your way. Then, get back in touch with who you are by actively investigating your likes and dislikes. Be wary of conforming too much or letting your critical thoughts get in the way of enjoying life. A healthy sense of self-worth includes accepting and embracing one' s individual tastes and interests.

WHAT I LIKE ABOUT MYSELF

Looking at the bright side of adolescence

What You' ll Need: Paper; pens; markers or colored pencils

Duration: 20 minutes

Best for: 2 to 6 people

LEADING THE ACTIVITY

1. Explain the importance of appreciating our strengths in building confidence.

2. Have everyone in the group name some good traits.

3. Have them sit quietly for a few minutes and think of and write down a list of their admirable traits.

4. Have them rate their most admired traits from one to ten on a scale.

5. Give them ten minutes to create a poster or script highlighting their best attributes to make the latter viral.

6. Have all the teens give a short speech about what makes them special.

7. Talk about the presentations you' ve seen.

DISCUSSION QUESTIONS

- Which admirable traits did most people share?

- Which admirable traits most stood out to you?

- How might remember all the positive things you' ve done help you now while things are tough?

PRO TIPS

- Teens will benefit from prompts as they consider examples of their excellent characteristics. For example, take the question, " In what ways do you make your family proud?" as an illustration.

- Shy teenagers may find it difficult to provide personal information. However, they should be pushed to make the poster and give the presentation nevertheless, with the suggestion that they enlist the aid of a more gregarious peer.

- If necessary, adjust the number of admirable traits teenagers are encouraged to rate.

PART 3: COGNITIVE BEHAVIORAL THERAPY

The effective psychological treatment of Cognitive Behavioral Therapy (CBT) , is grounded in a consistent, all-encompassing theory of associated emotions and behaviors. The hypothesis can help track the origins of each person' s unique emotional challenges. CBT tools derived from the theory and refined by practitioners over the past 40 years are equally important. With a wide range of options, therapists can meet their patient' s needs and cater to their preferences.

The efficacy of Cognitive Behavioral Therapy (CBT) stems from the fact that studies have already proven its benefits in treating many mental health conditions. This book contains tried-and-true techniques for helping you or your clients build resilience, positive thought patterns, and emotional control.

This book will show you how to radically revamp your relationships and mental health by changing the way you think. It won' t be simple, but you' ll immediately see a change. If you put the advice in these chapters into practice, you will see improvements in every aspect of your life.

The book is not about finding the silver lining in every situation. There is an equal distribution of good, bad, and ugly over one' s lifetime. We cannot remedy regular life' s difficulties by using magic. However, when you encounter a setback, you can retrain your brain to think differently and find a new solution.

Cognitive Behavior Therapy (CBT) is the method we' ll focus on throughout this book. Behavioral therapy that resembles CBT has been around for quite some time. It' s a simple approach that breaks down the causes and solutions to mental health issues, including stress, depression, and anxiety. Better yet, CBT has a solid scientific foundation. The method has proven to be effective.

Chapter 1: Definition of CBT

CBT is a highly structured, solution-focused, and brief method that employs various strategies to help patients gain more control over their emotions and actions, thereby reducing symptoms and enhancing their capacity to cope with life's stresses. The theoretical foundation of CBT incorporates early theories of behaviorism and cognition, or how people behave and how they learn and think, respectively. It aims to explain that our thoughts, not external circumstances, impact our emotions and actions and that we can exert greater control over them. The concept is that individuals and situations do not make us feel awful; instead, our judgments do.

Evidence-based methods have become a key criterion for judging the success of psychotherapy, and they are a crucial factor in the increasing acceptance and use of Cognitive Behavioral Therapy (CBT) . This approach has been tested and proved in research and real-world settings to deliver desired outcomes for customers.

The field of psychology has established that Cognitive Behavioral Therapy (CBT) is effective for treating:

- Depression

- Anxiety

- Obsessive-Compulsive Disorder (OCD) and intrusive thoughts

- Phobias

- Stress

- Addiction

- Procrastination

Cognitive Behavioral Therapy (CBT) raises one's self-esteem, makes one happier, and increases one's level of life satisfaction. CBT will help you see if you've been feeling trapped and confused about your next steps. You will gain insight into who you are, let go of the past, and look forward with optimism.

Chapter 2: The Theory behind CBT

In the 1960s, American psychiatrist Aaron Beck developed CBT in response to critiques of psychoanalysis that claimed the practice was not goal-oriented and did not pay enough attention to clients' thoughts in confidence. According to Beck, one's thoughts and perceptions are the driving forces behind one's emotions and actions. Ultimately, CBT aims to assist patients in seeing how their negative thought patterns contribute to their harmful actions.

Therefore, creating goals is critical for identifying which ideas and actions are more critical to help the client achieve the desired transformation. Cognitive Behavioral Therapy (CBT) goals accommodate each patient depending on their unique circumstances. Each CBT session should get the client closer to their objectives, as this is what makes the therapy so effective. Therefore, every activity or method involves goal-setting to develop a realistic and significant goal.

The Cognitive Triangle

CBT operates on the premise that internal processes, rather than external stimuli, determine how we act and react. The cognitive triangle, a simplified model of this idea used in CBT, asserts that thoughts affect feelings, behaviors and reactions, new feelings, and so on. Furthermore, because of the interrelated nature of ideas, emotions, and actions, a shift in any one will have ripple effects on the others. Using this approach, we can see that while we can't always choose whether or not we'll face a given challenge, we can decide how to react once we do.

Thoughts

Thought awareness is far more ephemeral than awareness of emotions or actions. Thoughts constantly flood our minds because of the infinite number of stimuli. The cognitive triangle shows how our beliefs influence our interpretations, shaping our emotions and behaviors.

FEELINGS

I can't count the number of people I've met who have told me they'd be able to alter their behavior or way of thinking if only they could eliminate unpleasant emotions. For instance, a person with a social phobia could think they might start making friends if only their phobia went away.

BEHAVIORS

Both our thoughts and our feelings are subject to random chance and are beyond our ability to control. However, the vast majority of our actions are under our control. Because our minds and hearts are so powerful, we don't always feel that way. Consider the most recent time you woke up and thought, "I don't want to work today." Nevertheless, you got dressed and went to work despite feeling uninspired and sluggish. Reactions are often voluntary regardless of one's internal state of mind.

The "B" in CBT is the many behavioral techniques that help us alter our internal mental state. Clients can learn helpful information about their underlying basic ideas and feelings through practice outside therapy, which we can use to evaluate and inform future therapy sessions. You can use the worksheets in this workbook to do this type of "homework."

THE KEY ASSUMPTIONS OF CBT

Any therapeutic approach rests on a foundation of assumptions. Consider these presumptions to be a mental structure model.

Practitioners of Cognitive Behavioral Therapy (CBT) hold the view that faulty ways of thinking (or false beliefs about oneself) are at the root of mental health issues (such as depression, anxiety, stress, and unhealthy behaviors). The stories we tell ourselves when we have irrational, negative ideas about ourselves, others, and the world, in general, ultimately cause us distress.

It's too simple to slip into the trap of repeatedly making the same logical mistakes. For instance, an individual suffering from depression is likely to view the world as a dark and terrible place with nothing to offer except misery. As a result, your outlook on life darkens, you avoid activities that boost your mood, and the cycle continues.

How we interpret the world affects our actions. A skewed perspective on the world makes it harder to respond to changes and difficulties in our surroundings and life. For example, you may be afraid to go outside because of the myths you tell yourself about the world, such as the fact that it is unsafe.

In addition, negative ideas can be identified and replaced. We may determine the specifics of our negative thought processes with the correct methods. As a result, we have the option of making a different decision. Concentrating on the present is more helpful than speculating on the causes of someone' s cognitive distortions, which may have their roots in the past.

A CBT therapist may inquire about the client' s upbringing to identify the origins of the latter' s negative core beliefs. You won' t need to go deep into your past to complete the tasks in this book. The focus is on immediate self-care for maximum efficiency.

While both cognitive and behavioral therapies have their histories, they complement one another well in clinical practice. Indeed, it wasn' t too long after the two approaches were developed and combined into CBT. Even cognitive therapy' s progenitor, Aaron T. Beck, rebranded his flagship method as " cognitive behavior therapy" to reflect the growing prominence of behavioral strategies within the field. Patients in need of care will benefit from this consolidation as they will access a more comprehensive range of services.

These treatments shed light on the interconnectedness of our emotions, thoughts, and actions when used together. Intense worry, for instance, can cause us to dwell on frightening possibilities, which only serves to heighten our sense of unease. As a result of these thoughts and sensations, we may try to avoid situations that trigger our fears, which only increases our anxiety. When we recognize these interrelationships, we can more easily implement solutions to improve our emotional well-being.

Most of CBT' s guiding ideas and procedures are unlikely to be novel to you. Overcoming our concerns by approaching them head-on is one such example that is rarely original. Patients I' ve worked with in the past were often unconvinced that seemingly simple methods like making itineraries and keeping track of ideas might assist them. They think they would have improved long ago if it were so easy. But, as we shall see, how we carry out CBT is just as important as the actions themselves. So, let' s take into account the positives of CBT.

Time-Limited

CBT is cost-effective and offers quick relief because a typical course of treatment is limited to a specific number of sessions, typically 12 to 16. In contrast, other modalities, like psychoanalysis, can include multiple sessions per week for several years. Furthermore, CBT effectively maximizes the client's time by relying on action-oriented at-home assignments and practice, similar to the exercises you will encounter in this workbook. In addition, occasional follow-up sessions can be helpful.

The skills taught usually improve people's ability to solve problems, socialize, and manage their emotions and time. CBT leads to long-term results that are often generalizable to other areas in life beyond the issues that initially led you or your client to seek help. Because clients know that CBT therapy has an endpoint and goals are specific and time-limited, this can be highly motivating and encouraging.

Here and Now

In contrast to other theoretical approaches, CBT is concerned with the " now and now" (" here and now" ?) regarding present difficulties rather than the past. Looking back may provide light on what went wrong, but it won' t help you deal with the current crisis. For example, if you drop a glass and it shatters on the floor, it' s more important to pick up the shards and ensure you don' t cut yourself than to analyze why the glass broke. So instead, Cognitive Behavioral Therapy (CBT) focuses on examining how one' s past has influenced their present-day ways of thinking and behaving, recognizing that early experiences impact current difficulties.

Concrete beliefs, or firmly held views about oneself, other people, and the world, are another form of mental baggage that Cognitive Behavioral Therapy (CBT) identifies as impacting one' s current way of thinking. Some of the exercises in this book shed light on how these ideas affect the big picture in our thinking.

Active Participation

Unlike other therapies, CBT has a directive, structured approach in that therapists show clients alternative ways of thinking and behaving. Although a CBT therapist or workbook provides specific techniques and strategies, meaningful progress requires active participation from the client to work collaboratively with the therapist and put in extra effort outside therapy. In addition, in-session experiences are essential for reviewing ideas, increasing insight into unhealthy patterns, and checking on progress.

But given the time constraint of therapy sessions, homework and exercises must be practiced outside therapy to help solidify new thinking patterns and develop practical coping skills. Therefore, it is highly engaging and holds the clients accountable for their personal growth. CBT is a big commitment; it takes persistence to apply newly acquired skills to real-world settings and improve your overall well-being.

HOMEWORK

CBT often includes homework as part of treatment. Clients of Cognitive Behavioral Therapists (CBTs) are frequently given homework assignments and asked to keep journals between sessions. For example, a therapist may have a new patient keep a mood diary for a week or have them write down their negative thoughts as often as possible. In addition, a few exercises at the end of each chapter will help you put what you've learned about CBT into practice.

Get a notebook and pen and have them handy before continuing. Date the page at the top right-hand corner each time you begin a new task or list. You are not required to share your study results with anyone. This notepad is strictly confidential. It's best to hide or lock it up if you share your home with others. If you hate writing, you could use a voice recorder or note-taking app on your phone or computer.

CBT PRINCIPLES

Before starting your trip, let's examine some of CBT's fundamental tenets. These will serve as a road map to efficient procedures.

Positive thinking is not the only goal of Cognitive Behavioral Therapy. Logic and reason are fundamental. We must accept it and decide what to do. The purpose of Cognitive Behavioral Therapy (CBT) is not to have you shut down your emotional responses. To put it simply, CBT is an emotional journey. The most straightforward approach to influencing your emotions is to change the way you' re thinking and acting. Therefore, this is where the focus lies.

The core tenet of Cognitive Behavioral Therapy is that we frequently err in our thinking, particularly regarding emotional reasoning. For example, imagine you' re anxious because a friend hasn' t returned your call or text. You may be drawing the wrong conclusion about your friend' s mood. Even though you don' t know what your friend is experiencing, you react emotionally to the assumption that your friend is upset with you. Perhaps you would stop talking to that person altogether or refuse to return their calls. The issue here is that there is no way to verify your suspicions or make amends if it turns out your friend was justified in being upset with you. Because of this, you may have lost a significant learning opportunity, and the problematic attitudes and actions remain unchanged.

CBT is most effective when you actively determine your treatment' s goals and develop a plan to achieve them. Collaboration is necessary to adjust the components of the treatment practice to your specific needs, whether directed by a therapist or a resource like this one. Defining the issue at hand is essential in cognitive behavioral therapy since it helps the patient feel more in control. Setting concrete, personally meaningful goals is integral to the therapeutic process. We' ll be able to channel our efforts and enthusiasm toward these targets.

While some therapies emphasize early experiences, cognitive behavioral therapy (CBT) centers on how current thoughts and behaviors can contribute to and even alleviate ongoing difficulties. Though CBT addresses critical learning events early in life, its emphasis on the present makes it an empowering treatment, concentrating on elements within our control. With CBT, you' ll learn a few fundamental skills to help you handle the challenges that brought you to treatment. With enough practice, you' ll be able to use these strategies independently, no matter what obstacles you encounter. Cognitive Behavioral Therapy (CBT) benefits continue to be useful even after therapy.

CBT emphasizes self-care and teaches clients skills to maintain their health. We can look for indicators of a recurrence of anxiety, depression, or other problems by tracing their roots to their causes. For instance, a woman who has overcome depression may recognize her predisposition to avoid the things that help her maintain her mental health. Due to these reasons, CBT has lower relapse rates for depression and anxiety than medication. Like a musician who wants to keep their skills sharp, someone who has undergone Cognitive Behavioral Therapy (CBT) must maintain their new routines through regular practice.

CBT achieves its desired effect of providing relief in a timely fashion. Fear of dogs, for instance, can be efficiently addressed in a session lasting two to four hours. At the same time, depression often requires a 16-session program. Shorter treatment programs can be motivational since they instill a sense of urgency in the job. CBT's components are delivered sequentially, with later sessions expanding upon and consolidating material offered in previous ones. Every session is structured the same way, beginning with a review of the client's practice between meetings, moving on to the topic at hand, and concluding with a strategy session for incorporating the content into the client's life moving forward. CBT's effectiveness stems in large part from its methodical methodology.

At the heart of CBT is the idea that our thoughts often lead us astray. Negative automatic thoughts, which arise on their own without any conscious effort on our part, are a common problem for human beings. Cognitive Behavioral Therapy (CBT) teaches you how to recognize and deal with such destructive thought patterns. For example, a man overlooked for a promotion may think unfavorably of himself and think, " I can never catch a break." Since negative automatic thoughts might occur underneath our awareness, the first step in CBT is learning to notice what the mind is saying to us. Then we examine the thoughts for accuracy. Finally, we can train our brains to think in more constructive ways.

An astonishing number of techniques fall under the CBT category, from relaxation training to cognitive restructuring to behavioral activation, exposure, and meditation. To a large extent, cognitive behavioral therapy consists of determining which treatment methods will be most beneficial to a given patient. In the following chapters, you'll be introduced to various such resources and learn which ones are most useful to you.

Chapter 3: Play Therapy and CBT

It has been well acknowledged that expressive arts and play materials are practical means of assisting children and adolescents with emotional and behavioral issues. Incorporating play approaches into CBT enables patients to express their difficulties through various non-threatening channels. Sand tray, miniature creatures and objects, clay and play dough, puppets, games, activities, and arts & crafts are some of the materials I employ. I also incorporate mindfulness into my work by utilizing appropriate practices for children and adolescents.

Young adult issues may include difficulty with peers, sexual or developmental concerns, school or work struggles, family disparities, etc. As they move from adolescence to adulthood, young individuals may benefit from the services of a therapist or other skilled mental health professional due to the quick and numerous changes that frequently characterize this phase.

Most physicians who treat children and adolescents believe that play therapy or play within therapy is vital to engaging children and adolescents in what is normally a more verbal activity, and CBT is no exception. In addition, play increases kids' participation in CBT's core therapies, particularly younger youths. For instance, an engaged and active child is more likely to benefit from the graduated exposures that are key to effective OCD therapy, and a depressed child is more likely to benefit from pleasurable activity scheduling if the child is engaged in this work and the treatment process in general.

However, there are significant distinctions between how play is regarded and utilized in CBT and traditional play therapy. In conventional play therapy, the therapist observes the child's psychological development without leading or influencing them. Traditional play therapists consider direction as a sort of control and non-acceptance of the young, believing that youth will work through their problems via play without direction or influence. Therefore, the play therapist does not actively praise, instruct, or educate children because these activities are viewed as managing children and the psychological process. In CBT, however, the therapist actively uses play to lead youth through treatment activities and phases.

Central tasks of CBT include praise, rewards, psychoeducation, and actively teaching youth skills, and play supports the implementation of these tasks. In traditional play therapy, play is the therapy, whereas, in CBT, play is used to engage the child in therapy tasks and goals.

Play is essential to all aspects of cognitive behavioral therapy, including assessment, psychoeducation, treatment tactics, exposure tasks, and relapse prevention. For instance, during the evaluation phase, the therapist may urge young patients to use a puppet to reveal their difficult or humiliating thoughts instead of directly disclosing these thoughts to the therapist. Likewise, throughout the relapse prevention phase, the youth and therapist may produce a song or tale or draw a picture that illustrates the most important lessons acquired during therapy.

Chapter 4: General CBT Activities

In this chapter, we will look at various cutting-edge CBT tools that we can adapt to treat many mental health issues. It is highly encouraged to work through each exercise as the strategies build on one another. There is a large variety of abilities to choose from, and they are categorized in ways that make it easy to identify the ones that are most applicable to your situation. By the time you finish this chapter, you will have a list of your favorite skills.

Some cognitive-based exercises may help you become more conscious of your ideas and start to form a knowledge of adaptive strategies for changing them. You'll then use your newly acquired knowledge of the cognitive triangle by tracking and monitoring techniques to keep tabs on your mood, reactions, and triggers. Finally, you will learn about thought distortions and strategies to confront and rectify them through cognitive restructuring once you have developed the skills necessary to observe and track the relationships among triggers, ideas, feelings, and behaviors.

Identifying Automatic Thoughts

Our thoughts significantly affect our disposition and actions. Thoughts might be welcomed when we know what we're thinking about exactly, or they can sneak up on us when we have no idea what we're thinking. A lot of the time, the thoughts that impact you most are the ones that make you feel bad. We refer to these disruptive musings as negative automatic thoughts (NATs). To better control your emotions and actions, it helps to have the skill of recognizing and labeling certain types of ideas.

Instruction:

Thinking about when you felt nervous, unhappy, or disturbed can help you cope with those feelings later in the day or within a few hours of first becoming aware of them.

Find the feeling that was a catalyst, and then figure out what happened. There are various triggers for emotional responses. Sadness, for instance, is a common reaction to disappointment, loss, or the end of a relationship.

Dig further into the significance of the circumstances and the feelings involved. Ask yourself thoughtful questions to unearth previously concealed ideas. For instance, you may wonder, " If they didn' t offer me the job, what does it mean?" If there is a negative aspect, what is it, and why is it so bad? Just what does that imply about me?

EXAMPLE

TRIGGER	Friend does not invite me to their party
EMOTION	Sad, angry, hurt, disappointed
THOUGHTS	They don' t want me to come. They don' t like me.
MEANING	I never get invited to parties because I' m not enough.

EVENT ONE

TRIGGER	
EMOTION	
THOUGHTS	
MEANING	

EVENT TWO

TRIGGER	
EMOTION	
THOUGHTS	
MEANING	

REVIEW

Can you tell the difference between how aware you are of your emotions and thoughts?

_____

Do you identify any recurring themes?

_____

Were there any more inquiries into meaning that you discovered?

_____

IDENTIFYING TRIGGERS

A trigger is a stimulus that contributes to undesirable responses. For example, being in a large crowd can make us feel worried and unpleasant. The conditions are not the issue; nevertheless, our thoughts may be. Because we incorrectly associate our thoughts and perceptions with the conditions that generate them, we tend to blame our triggers for how we feel or react.

The purpose of this exercise is to assist you in distinguishing your perceptions from your triggers, understanding their impact on your moods and behaviors, and developing better strategies to deal with them.

INSTRUCTION:

Try considering the following groups of triggers while you think about yours. Don't dismiss random ideas that cross your mind. Triggers can be tied to anything, not just people, locations, or objects (for example, social media) . Please list your triggers on the accompanying chart.

EMOTIONAL STATE	
PEOPLE	
PLACES	
THINGS	
THOUGHTS	
ACTIVITIES/ SITUATIONS	

IDENTIFYING AND MONITORING EMOTIONS

Although we frequently wish we could, it is not beneficial to suppress negative feelings. Since emotions are designed to have us take some sort of action, they have considerable sway over our choices. However, understanding our feelings isn' t always a walk in the park.

We can feel a wide range of emotions at once, and it' s easy to mistake one for the other. Feelings are emotions that accompany specific bodily experiences; it' s important to train yourself to recognize them.

As a result, you' ll be able to tune in to your feelings and free yourself from destructive mental patterns.

MOODS THAT FIT THE FACTS CHART

FEAR	You feel a threat to your life or well-being or that of someone you care about.
ANGER	A vital goal is blocked. You or someone you care about is insulted, threatened, or hurt by others.
DISGUST	Someone you are in contact with contaminates you. Being around someone whose behavior could damage or harm you or a group you are part of.

ENVY	Another person has things you don't have but that you want.
JEALOUSY	You feel threatened that a relationship or object may be in danger, damaged, or taken away from you.
LOVE	You experience an inner fullness that deeply enhances your quality of life.
SADNESS	You lost something or someone. The expectations you have are not met.
SHAME	You feel rejected by others due to your characteristics or behaviors.
GUILT	Your behavior violates your morals.

Instructions: For the next week or more, think about how you react when confronted with negative feelings. Maintain a daily mood log using the space provided below.

DATE	SITUATION Describe what happened and not your thoughts about the situation	EMOTION AND INTENSITY (1 TO 10)	DO YOUR EMOTIONS FIT THE FACTS?

THOUGHT RECORD

Perception is the medium by which we engage the external world. Inappropriate feelings and actions may result from erroneous assumptions or interpretations. This is a time where keeping mental diaries come in handy.

Keeping a journal of your thoughts might help you become more self-aware of the connections between thoughts, emotions, and actions. However, to correct erroneous assumptions, you must first become aware of their connection.

SITUATION	THOUGHTS	EMOTIONS	BEHAVIORS	ALTERNATIVE THOUGHT

Challenging Negative Automatic Thoughts (NATs)

NATs can make people feel out of control and harm their emotions and actions. You could develop anxiety and depression if you give in to unrestrained ruminating about these matters. This activity is designed to help you recognize and alter NATs by providing a framework to examine your mental processes and triggers more dispassionately. You can use these questions to test yourself and other NATs in regular life.

Instructions:

Write your situational description in the " Situation" field. Write the NAT prompted by this event in the " Thought" field. To further evaluate your opinions, please respond to the following questions. Justify your position.

SITUATION	THOUGHT

Is there strong proof to back up this claim? Just what proof is there?

_____

Do you know of any evidence that contradicts this theory? In that case, could you please explain it?

_____

Am I making assumptions about the situation without sufficient information?

_____

Could it be that I'm misreading the evidence? Can you assume anything about me?

_____

When I think about this, how much of it is based on facts and how much on intuition?

_____

Is this a likely or worst-case scenario, in your opinion?

_____

Consider a friend's perspective: how do they see this?

_____

How does my optimistic, pessimistic, or agnostic perspective change anything?

_____

Will any of this even matter in a year? In five years?

_____

Identifying Thought Distortions

Distortions in our thought processes are habitual ways of thinking that lead us to incorrect conclusions about ourselves, others, and the world around us. Our emotions and actions can be impacted by our thought patterns, which are most often negative, judgmental, and rigid.

Although everyone occasionally encounters skewed thinking, those with mental health disorders may hold more extreme versions of distorted views and struggle more than others to think more rationally. Through a deeper understanding of how your mind works, you will be better able to control negative feelings and actions.

Instructions:

Take a look at this Thought Distortion Diagram. Then, under each prompt, indicate if you engage in this form of cognitive distortion by circling Yes or No. Then, in the blank spaces provided, please describe the circumstances that tend to cause this distortion in your thinking.

THOUGHT DISTORTION	MEANING	EXAMPLES
ALL-OR-NOTHING THINKING	Seeing things in absolutes or "black and white."	I never get asked out on a date.
OVERGENERALIZATION	Concluding one experience and generalizing to all experiences	I always have to be the one to reach out.
MENTAL FILTERS	Dwelling on a single negative detail leads to inaccurate perceptions	I received a low rating in one section of my review. I'm not valued.
LABELING	Name-calling or labeling yourself as if it is the truth	I'm not smart; I'm a loser.
SHOULD STATEMENTS	Criticizing yourself over things you think you should be or do	I should've graduated by now.
FORTUNE-TELLING	Making predictions	No one is going to talk to me.

MIND READING	Concluding that someone perceives you negatively	They think I'm boring.
EMOTIONAL REASONING	Reasoning with your feelings to come to conclusions or interpretations	I feel worried, so it's not going to work out.
COMPARISON GAME	Comparing your circumstance to others and feeling inferior	They moved out of their parents' home. I should have, too.
DISCOUNTING THE POSITIVE	Rejecting or ignoring positive experiences by discounting them	I passed because the test was easy.
CATASTROPHIZING	Focusing on the worst-case scenario,	She's going to break up with me.

All-or-nothing thinking: ☐ Yes ☐   No

Situation: _____

Overgeneralization: ☐   Yes ☐   No

Situation: _____

Mental filters: ☐ Yes ☐   No

Situation: _____

Labeling: ☐ Yes ☐   No

Situation: _____

Should statements: ☐ Yes ☐   No

Situation: _____

Fortune-telling: ☐ Yes ☐   No

Situation: _____

Mind reading: ☐ Yes ☐ No

Situation: _____

Emotional reasoning: ☐ Yes ☐ No

Situation: _____

Comparison game: ☐ Yes ☐ No

Situation: _____

Discounting the positive: ☐ Yes ☐ No

Situation: _____

Catastrophizing: ☐ Yes ☐ No

Situation: _____

CREATING A NEW NARRATIVE

Negative automatic thoughts can have good emotional and behavioral impacts when challenged. However, it is frequently more challenging to change deeply ingrained underlying ideas.

It may be necessary to dissect the circumstances that led to the problem and highlight data supporting the new viewpoint to make a lasting positive shift. This activity is designed to get you thinking about how you can rewrite your life story.

INSTRUCTIONS:

Put a self-belief on paper that you'd like to alter. Subsequently, jot down the new conviction that ought to take its place. Then, for a week, at the end of each day, jot down something that either supports your new belief or is not consistent with the previous belief (an event, something someone says to you, fresh insight, etc.) , and then indicate whether it is consistent or inconsistent with the old belief (C/ I) .

Old (self-critical) belief:

New (positive) belief:

Daily Gratitude Log

Daily acts of appreciation alter negative mental patterns and foster more optimistic perspectives on life. Daily thankfulness practices have improved mood and reduced negative distorted thinking.

Instructions: Keep a gratitude journal and record three daily things you're thankful for. It all counts, no matter how minute.

Sunday _____

Monday _____

Tuesday _____

Wednesday _____

Thursday _____

Friday _____

Saturday _____

Setting Self-Care Intentions

Not the situations themselves, but how we choose to perceive them, is the source of most of the difficulties we face. However, it's important to remember that there are other considerations beyond what we have thought and perceived.

If you spend too long without eating, for instance, you may find that your mood and thus your perspective shift negatively. Self-care is beneficial because it enhances health, fosters optimism, and makes us more resilient to stress. This activity is meant to help you recognize opportunities to take better care of yourself and then encourage you to implement those plans.

INSTRUCTIONS:

Examine how you now take care of yourself. Has anything I' ve done improved my emotional and physical health? Is there something I' m missing?

Consider your current self-care approach and list areas in which you' d like to see improvement.

TYPES OF SELF-CARE BEHAVIORS	EXAMPLE	MY SELF-CARE IDEAS
SLEEP	Seven to eight hours a night	
MOVEMENT/ EXERCISE	Move body three or four times a week.	
NUTRITION	Limit processed foods.	
PHYSICAL HEALTH	Yearly checkup. Schedule doctor appointments to address discomfort or pain.	
SUBSTANCE USE	Pay attention to the influence of substances on physical/ mental health—Limit alcohol, marijuana, caffeine, etc.	
DAILY ROUTINE/ STRUCTURE	Set wake/ sleep times. Schedule adequate time throughout the day for arriving on time, breaks, etc.	
OTHER SELF-CARE BEHAVIORS	Reflect on your behaviors on your good mental health days.	

1) Right now, I practice the following forms of self-care:

_____

2) Self-care practices I'd like to begin.

_____

3) Plan to engage in just one or two self-care activities you listed in the preceding entry. Foremost in achieving any goal is beginning at a possible minor level.

_____

4) Document Your Daily Routine. Consider the time of day, the location, and the amount of time needed for preparation.

_____

How to Do What You Say You're Going to Do

Get help from your friends and family. Pass the word to your loved ones to up the ante on accountability. Recruit help or get their backing by making this request.

Use a journal or app to keep tabs on your development.

Use self-compassion. Never settle for less than the best. Be aware of any critical ideas you may be having about yourself.

Weekly Behavioral Activation

By establishing manageable daily objectives, behavioral activation provides a framework for success. Positive mental and emotional states can be facilitated by accomplishing these aims. You need to break down the tasks into manageable chunks to prevent becoming overwhelming.

When you've proven that you can stick to and achieve basic objectives, you can start adding layers of complexity to your work. For example, behavioral activation aims to break people out of their habitual patterns of responding to rewards and punishments by enhancing their motivation and exposing them to more favorable experiences.

INSTRUCTIONS:

Just one, two, or three goals for each morning, afternoon, and night should be recorded in the chart below.

DAY	MORNING	AFTERNOON	EVENING
EXAMPLE	●Wake up at 8: 30 a.m. ●Brush teeth and wash face	●Read for 30 minutes	●Eat dinner by 7 p.m. ●Text one friend
MONDAY			
TUESDAY			
WEDNESDAY			
THURSDAY			
FRIDAY			
SATURDAY			
SUNDAY			

BEHAVIORAL EXPERIMENTS

Our disposition and actions will mirror our beliefs. Therefore, it's important to keep an eye out for unreasonable assumptions and the absence of proof to the contrary. Behavioral experiments provide an objective means of putting our presumptions and ideas to the test and making an informed determination as to whether or not the feelings and actions that follow are warranted.

INSTRUCTIONS:

Choose an irrational thought. Plan a means to test it using the following rules, and then carry out the experiment. Once finished, assess the experience and evidence to see if the original thought was correct or if it needs to be replaced.

PLAN EXPERIMENT

Thought to Test

Describe the thought, belief, or assumption you want to test.

_____

_____

_____

Experiment

How can you test this thought? When do you plan to execute?

_____

_____

_____

Prediction

What do you think will happen during this experiment? Do you expect any thought distortions? How distressed do you think you felt during the experiment on a scale of 1 to 10 (10 being the most distressed) ?

_____

_____

_____

After the experiment, answer the questions that follow Evaluate Results.

EVALUATE RESULTS

Results

What happened during the experiment? Were your predictions correct? Did you come to any different conclusions?

_____

_____

_____

New Conclusions

Given the evidence of this experiment, what is your new thought? Did it change or stay the same?

_____

_____

_____

Discussion

How do you feel after the experiment, on a scale of 1 to 10 (10 being the most distressed) ?

_____

_____

_____

DECATASTROPHIZING

Catastrophizing is a thinking distortion that accentuates difficulties or irrationally forecasts the worst-case situation. You can rectify cognitive distortions by decatastrophizing and questioning your thoughts.

INSTRUCTIONS:

Complete the following exercises.

What is the issue, and what are you concerned about? Change any "what ifs" to "I am concerned..."

_____

_____

_____

On a scale of 1 to 10, rate how terrible you believe this disaster will be if it occurs (10 being the most awful) .

How probable is the worst-case scenario to occur in reality? Give examples from your previous experience or other verifiable facts.

_____

_____

_____

What is the worst that could happen if the worst-case scenario occurs? What is the ideal scenario? What do you think a buddy would predict?

_____

_____

_____

What would you do if your worst-case scenario came true?

_____

_____

_____

What do you believe is the most likely outcome?

_____

_____

_____

What are the possibilities that you will be concerned about the outcome if the worst-case scenario occurs?

_____

_____

_____

PRACTICING MINDFULNESS

We often get caught up in attempting to change uncomfortable thoughts and emotions; mindfulness helps us to create a different connection with them. To practice mindfulness, one must focus on their present-moment thoughts and sensations on purpose.

Review the following methods and select three (one from each category) to practice for 2-10 minutes each this week.

MINDFULNESS EVERY DAY

Focusing on one' s senses while going about daily activities is a great way to train oneself to be more mindful and present. This activity includes employing one' s sense of touch, taste, sight, sound, and smell. For example, if you practice being attentive while washing the dishes, you will exercise awareness of the temperature of the water, the smell of the soap, the sound of running water, etc.

Mindfulness training can also be applied while doing daily household chores and activities.

"5-4-3-2-1" Grounding

Stop for a second and take in your immediate surroundings. Acknowledge five senses of sight, four of touch, three of sound, two of smell, and one of taste.

Mindfulness Walk or Passenger Ride

While you' re out for a stroll or ride (but not behind the wheel) , tune into how your body is feeling. Then pay attention to what you see, hear, or smell.

Chapter 5: CBT for Specific Issues

5.1 Anxiety

Putting Your Fear into Words

Explain what you fear the most and why in a single sentence.

You can use this exercise to begin therapy by identifying something you fear (such as " I am terrified of speaking to people I don' t know," " I am afraid of cats," or " I am afraid of visiting the dentist") and writing it down.

Once you identify the source of your anxiety, you may begin to develop strategies to overcome it.

Make a Fear Ladder

Create your own " fear ladder" by following the instructions above. Think of five to ten different scenarios. Don' t fudge the details.

For example, if you have a fear of elevators, do you also have a fear of using them in places like office buildings and shopping malls? Do you fear going up or down a single flight of stairs, three flights, or an entire building?

If you suffer from social anxiety and are afraid of talking to new people, here is what your fear ladder may look like. The least distressing thing on the list is #1, and the most frightening is #10.

Visualize Calm

If you' re feeling anxious, try visualizing a peaceful scene. Maybe you can see yourself on a beach towel, or perhaps you' re beside a waterfall, or maybe you' re in the middle of a forest, or maybe you' re in your bedroom. There are several possible environments to achieve this state of relaxation; select the one that best suits you. When dealing with generalized anxiety, this physical activity is highly effective.

Instructions:

Find a quiet spot, set a timer, and complete the following tasks.

1. Find a comfortable position on your bed, yoga mat, or the floor. Just close your eyes and think about a peaceful environment.

2. Imagine a peaceful place inside of you, place one hand on your tummy, and breathe in through your nose and out through your mouth.

3. To center yourself, put your bare feet on the floor or your body on the bed. (Anxiety can make a person feel like " they' re out of their body" ; thus, practicing grounding techniques might be beneficial.) You exist at this precise time and place.

4. When the alarm sounds, you should open your eyes. You may carry that calm with you as you go about your day. Recall that peaceful area whenever anxiety threatens. Stop worrying and create some calm in your mind.

In what location did you find peace? Tell me about the emotions and thoughts that arose during your visualization. Take note of any cognitive distortions and consider how you could reframe them.

_____

_____

_____

_____

_____

_____

_____

_____

_____

_____

_____

SING OUT YOUR ANXIETY

Feelings can be beautifully conveyed through music. Anxiety causes a buildup of nervous energy that needs an outlet. Examining your anxious thoughts and sensations may not always help. And that' s where singing comes in handy. Singing (and humming) can help you deal with challenging emotions. In other words, it' s a method for dealing with your feelings.

Additionally, even though you' re using the same words, your ideas' mood can shift when you sing. As a result, anxiety might be " defused" by singing, creating mental space for it. This activity is designed to facilitate the expression of inner emotions.

Instructions: Sing loudly or hum the tune while you wash your hair. If singing in the shower makes you uncomfortable, try it while driving or just out and about. What other people think of you is none of your business. Focusing on action rather than analysis is key to success in this endeavor.

The tunes are entirely up to you. Some people find that listening to furious music helps them release their anxieties. Perhaps you' ll pair your nervous musings with a lively rock tune. Don' t let your worries get the best of you; instead, channel that nervous energy into a song about your frustrations. You can sing your worrying ideas out loud.

You can rap about your thoughts or write a poem about them. If you can separate your thoughts from your identity, you may find them less intimidating. In any case, you' ll probably feel more stable and relaxed afterward.

How did you feel after singing your chosen song? Was there a noticeable difference between thinking and singing the same thing?

_____

_____

_____

_____

_____

_____

5.2 Depression

Completing Sentences

When you engage in sentence completion activities, you can better identify limiting self-schemas and overcome them.

Write down the following sentences as they are completed for you. Overthinking will get in the way. Just start writing anything that pops into your head.

As a person, " I am the type who..."

My life has taught me that the world is..."

Thinking ahead, I can' t help but wonder..."

This sort of mental activity can yield some surprising insights. Finding out how pessimistic your outlook has grown may come as a shock to you.

Negative self-schemas may keep you mired in a never-ending downward spiral of despair. Suppose you have a pessimistic outlook and believe that nothing will ever improve. In that case, you might not try to establish plans or achieve your goals.

Self-Critical Monitoring Log

Intrusive, distressing negative ideas about one' s self are a hallmark symptom of depression; while depressed, we pay extra attention to these thoughts and focus on information that confirms these views, which in turn impact our actions and heighten our sadness, isolation, and guilt.

To criticize oneself means to point out one' s shortcomings. While being aware of where you may improve is helpful, it can also lead to erroneous beliefs that sap your sense of value, confidence, and desire to get out there and do things. Being able to recognize and question negative ideas about oneself is a crucial first step in learning to cope with depression.

Instructions:

Do some introspection and journaling after each day or whenever you become aware of having critical or otherwise negative thoughts about yourself or your life.

SITUATION	EMOTIONS AND BODY SENSATIONS	SELF-CRITICAL/ NEGATIVE THOUGHTS	COPING RESPONSES	ALTERNATIVE RESPONSE

MOOD TRACKER

When depressed, people withdraw from their activities and social circles, worsening their condition. Social interaction and increased exercise can alleviate depressive symptoms, although depressed persons often resist these approaches. Keeping track of your emotions might help you identify the causes of any distress you may be experiencing.

Instructions: For the following week, keep track of how you' re feeling emotionally (happy, sad, anxious, etc.) and what' s happening around that time. Doing so can help you identify correlations between your current circumstances and past feelings.

	7 A.M. TO 10 A.M.	10 A.M. TO 1 P.M.	1 P.M. TO 4 P.M.	4 P.M. TO 7 P.M.	7 P.M. TO 10 P.M.	10 P.M. TO 1 A.M.	1 A.M. TO 7 A.M.
MONDAY							
TUESDAY							
WEDNESDAY							
THURSDAY							
FRIDAY							
SATURDAY							
SUNDAY							

NOTES:

_____

_____

_____

_____

_____

_____

_____

_____

_____

_____

_____

_____

Thought-Restructuring Record

Distorted thought patterns and repetitive patterns of self-critical thoughts create a breeding ground for depression to wreak havoc on relationships, health, and work productivity.

Instructions:

Use the following chart to keep track of your thoughts and feelings regarding depression throughout the day or whenever you notice them. Continue to the next section and respond to the questions there. Make copies of the chart and refer to it whenever you feel your mood beginning to dip.

SITUATION	DEPRESSIVE/ SELF -CRITICAL THOUGHTS	FEELINGS AND SENSATIONS INTENSITY (0 TO 10)	BEHAVIORS

Thought-Restructuring Questions

Here are some questions to help you analyze and improve your thinking. It could be useful to start by responding to all of the questions.

In contrast, when it becomes simpler to question and generate new ideas, you may only need to ask yourself a few questions to reframe your perspective completely.

Do you have any solid proof to back up this claim?

_____

_____

_____

Can you point to any relevant evidence that contradicts this theory?

_____

_____

_____

What is the way that I would like to interpret this matter?

_____

_____

_____

Do any cognitive distortions exist? Please describe them and think about how to alter these perspectives.

_____

_____

_____

What would a true friend say to me if they weren' t going to judge me?

_____

_____

_____

Are there any positive feelings or memories that I could be hiding from myself?

_____

_____

_____

Can I find anything positive in this circumstance?

_____

_____

_____

Is there a fresh perspective we can take on this matter?

_____

_____

_____

What are these brand-new emotions? (Judge their seriousness.)

_____

_____

_____

Could there be another approach to this?

_____

_____

_____

IDENTIFYING RESILIENCY FACTORS

Depression makes it easier to ignore resilient variables over which we may have some control and instead focus on the perceived problem triggers and scenarios. These things make us more resilient to the pressures of daily life.

If you don' t eat regularly or stick to a schedule, you may start to feel angry and lazy, which might cloud your judgment. However, sleep, exercise, physical health, consistent daily routines, and self-care practices are all resiliency variables that can be tuned into to build a healthy environment to battle the maladaptive thinking and behavior that characterizes depression.

Instructions: Consider the following list of strengths that can help you bounce back from adversity. Try to evaluate yourself and determine where you may use improvement. Please rate each topic from 1 to 5, with 5 being the most urgent. Next, please answer the following questions to work together to establish practical, attainable objectives or practices.

TYPES OF SELF-CARE BEHAVIORS	SITUATIONS YOU FIND YOURSELF IN	NEED ATTENTION (0 TO 5)
SLEEP		
MOVEMENT/ EXERCISE		

NUTRITION		
PHYSICAL HEALTH		
SUBSTANCE USE		
DAILY ROUTINE/ STRUCTURE		
SOCIAL SUPPORT		
HOBBIES/ PLEASURABLE ACTIVITIES		
OTHER SELF-CARE BEHAVIORS		

1. What are the three most pressing concerns you have?

_____

_____

_____

2. Make a list of three of your most important areas, and include one specific behavior or objective from each. Consider the time of day, the location, and the time needed to get ready for each objective, and then make a concrete strategy.

_____

_____

_____

3. Where can you find one to three persons to contact?

_____

_____

POSITIVE DAILY LOG

Keeping a positive notebook will help you generate fresh perspectives on your daily activities to clear out skewed thought processes.

Instructions: For the next week, please take a few minutes to reflect on three good things that happened that day and answer the questions below. It should take between 5 and 10 minutes to complete each submission. No detail is too insignificant. Coffee, a hilarious commercial, or a stroll in the park are all great topics for a writing prompt.

POSITIVE EXPERIENCES DAY 1 DATE _____	WHY WAS THIS A POSITIVE EXPERIENCE?	HOW CAN I RE-CREATE THIS EXPERIENCE?
1. _____	_____	_____
2. _____	_____	_____
3. _____	_____	_____
POSITIVE EXPERIENCES DAY 2 DATE _____	WHY WAS THIS A POSITIVE EXPERIENCE?	HOW CAN I RE-CREATE THIS EXPERIENCE?
1. _____	_____	_____
2. _____	_____	_____
3. _____	_____	_____
POSITIVE EXPERIENCES DAY 3 DATE _____	WHY WAS THIS A POSITIVE EXPERIENCE?	HOW CAN I RE-CREATE THIS EXPERIENCE?
1. _____	_____	_____
2. _____	_____	_____

3. _____	_____	_____
POSITIVE EXPERIENCES DAY 4 DATE _____	**WHY WAS THIS A POSITIVE EXPERIENCE?**	**HOW CAN I RE-CREATE THIS EXPERIENCE?**
1. _____	_____	_____
2. _____	_____	_____
3. _____	_____	_____
POSITIVE EXPERIENCES DAY 5 DATE _____	**WHY WAS THIS A POSITIVE EXPERIENCE?**	**HOW CAN I RE-CREATE THIS EXPERIENCE?**
1. _____	_____	_____
2. _____	_____	_____
3. _____	_____	_____
POSITIVE EXPERIENCES DAY 6 DATE _____	**WHY WAS THIS A POSITIVE EXPERIENCE?**	**HOW CAN I RE-CREATE THIS EXPERIENCE?**
1. _____	_____	_____
2. _____	_____	_____
3. _____	_____	_____
POSITIVE EXPERIENCES DAY 7 DATE _____	**WHY WAS THIS A POSITIVE EXPERIENCE?**	**HOW CAN I RE-CREATE THIS EXPERIENCE?**
1. _____	_____	_____
2. _____	_____	_____
3. _____	_____	_____

5.3 STRESS

MEDITATION AND OBSERVATION

Instructions: Make space to be alone with your anxious thoughts and sensations. Sit down, close your eyes, and concentrate on your breathing.

1. Choose a place to sit where you can relax and close your eyes.

2. Inhale deeply four times through your nose and exhale completely four times through your mouth.

3. Pay attention to the physical manifestations of stress. Tension in specific muscles is a common physical manifestation of stress.

4. Simply inhale deeply through your nose four times and exhale completely through your mouth.

5. Let your mind wander.

6. Imagine your thoughts to be clouds passing through the sky.

7. Take four slow, deep breaths through your nose and then out through your mouth.

8. Take a moment to re-evaluate where the strain is manifesting physically.

9. Do Steps 2-8 again.

10. After twenty minutes, you may not feel relieved of stress, but you should feel more centered and at peace.

Respond to the following questions:

Where did you feel the strain on your body?

_____

_____

_____

Consider your thoughts: what did you notice?

_____

_____

_____

Did you find that releasing your ideas helped you relax? In that case, why?

_____

_____

_____

How did you feel when you let go of your body' s sensations? If that' s the case, why would you think that?

_____

_____

_____

PRACTICE 5-5-5 BREATHING

Instructions: Relax in a chair, on the floor, or in any other comfortable position. Take a deep breath in and out as you mentally count to five. Then, repeatedly count to five as you exhale. You must first wait five seconds before taking another breath.

As you focus on your breathing, you' ll naturally feel calmer. Since you were already anxious before starting this routine, it' s natural that anxious ideas would flood your head. Take note of the thoughts, but reassure yourself that you don' t have to act on them. All you have to do here is breathe.

IDENTIFY STRESS TRIGGERS

Sometimes, what stresses us out isn' t a single major event but rather a confluence of many minor ones. You get an immediate onset of a feeling that can only be described as " stressed out." A lot is happening, most of it routine and common. Yet here you are, at a breaking point, and you have no idea how you got here. Consider how you might reduce your exposure to potential stressors. You may be putting too much emphasis on yourself.

Instructions:

When you say, " I' m so stressed," it' s important to take a break and answer the following questions:

What precipitated the current crisis? What did you think before you told yourself that you were stressed out? Just before you made that remark, what were you thinking? Maybe you were feeling anxious, and thoughts like, " I' ll never get this done in five hours," crossed your mind.

_____

_____

_____

I' m curious as to what gave rise to those ideas. Perhaps you' re putting too much pressure on yourself to finish in five hours when the activity could take longer.

_____

_____

_____

Are there specific beliefs you held that catalyzed stress? For example, perhaps it was some variation on the theme of " I' ll have let everyone down if I don' t do this," " I' m a horrible failure," or " I never finish anything on time."

_____

_____

Find the distorted thinking behind these beliefs and correct them.

_____

_____

_____

Think of something that strikes a better balance. Is there any genuine danger if you don' t finish the project in five hours?

_____

_____

_____

5.4 IMPROVING COMMUNICATION SKILLS

ACTIVELY LISTEN AND DEBUNK MIND READING

People frequently presume they know the other person' s thoughts. However, no one can genuinely read the minds of others. You may have a decent understanding of how someone feels and what they are thinking based on their actions, facial expressions, and body language.

But you cannot know what someone thinks if they do not express them. This situation is extremely difficult, if not impossible, via email and text due to the lack of nonverbal indicators and tone of voice.

Time: 15 minutes

Format: Conversation and written exercise

Instructions: Ask a close friend to complete this activity with you (see the tip at the end of the exercise) . Partner A will be one individual, and Partner B will be another.

Before starting, please respond to the following questions:

Who do you wish to perform this activity with?

_____

_____

_____

How do you believe this strategy will enhance this relationship? What, if any, modifications would you like to see?

_____

_____

_____

Now commence the exercise. Partner A remains mute while Partner B expresses their emotions. Partner A writes on a separate sheet of paper what they heard Partner B say and what they believe Partner B is thinking. On a separate sheet of paper, Partner B records their true thoughts. Then, compare your respective writings.

Next, switch positions. Doing so will help you pay close attention to one another and likely demonstrate that neither of you can read the mind of the other.

Ask the individual whether they would want to complete this exercise with you. If they reject your request, jot down how you feel.

Is there any cognitive distortion? Keep in mind that not everyone is comfortable performing therapeutic exercises. Choose someone else to ask.

PRACTICE IN FRONT OF THE MIRROR

When you want your voice to be heard and your views effectively communicated to others, you must first be familiar with your voice and body language. The mirror exercise is an effective method for this. Practicing in front of a mirror can help you make modifications and become more comfortable expressing yourself in various settings.

Time: 10 to 15 minutes

Format: Observation, verbal practice, and writing exercise

Instructions:

1. Observe your reflection in a full-length mirror while standing in front of it. Stand erect but not stiff (try to be comfortable) , with your chin and shoulders back (not slumped) , and make eye contact.

2. Communicate with your reflection as if you were a person with whom you wish to communicate a purpose. It may be someone with whom you want to set a boundary or someone you meet at a party with whom you want to discuss. Remind yourself that you are safe and can freely express your thoughts and emotions to the mirror without fear of criticism. Remind yourself that you possess the right to be heard.

3. Be mindful of your body language as you practice communicating calmly. Make necessary adjustments to your tone of voice and posture.

4. After completing the exercise, which can be applied to various situations, please respond to the following questions.

How and why did this workout make you feel?

_____

_____

_____

What were you contemplating? Are there any cognitive distortions that could be reframed?

_____

_____

_____

What was the most profound or unexpected thing you said to yourself during the exercise?

_____

_____

_____

What is the significance of this specific statement?

_____

_____

_____

SET BOUNDARIES

If you do not set limits with others, they may be unaware of your preferences and limitations; this can leave you feeling bitter and increase your negative relationship-related thought patterns.

Time: 10 to 15 minutes

Format: Conversation

Instructions: Consider the persons you routinely engage with and what you deem acceptable and unacceptable in their behavior toward you. The things you find unacceptable are the boundaries you must establish and communicate.

Perhaps your friend urges you to go to late-night dancing clubs, but you're not into that environment, and she tries to convince you otherwise. You acknowledge her position (she believes it will be enjoyable) but disagree. It is time to take a stand. The " stand your ground" strategy operates as follows:

1. Summarize the individual's emotions. (For example, " I know you enjoy going to clubs to dance, and that would be enjoyable for you.")

2. Explain your disagreement and why you cannot comply with their request. (For instance, " I dislike dancing clubs, and I would not find it enjoyable.")

3. Suggest an alternative. (For instance, " I' d love to see a movie with you. We can both choose a movie to watch.") Thus, you may maintain your boundaries while granting your friend the social time she desires.

Respond to the prompts below:

Identify a boundary you wish to establish with someone and explain why it is vital.

_____

_____

_____

What alternative do you suggest?

_____

_____

_____

What negative things come to mind when you consider putting a limit? Existence of cognitive distortions? If so, attempt to reframe them.

_____

_____

_____

ANALYZE YOUR SOCIAL NETWORK

Many individuals do not evaluate their connections; this can lead to unintentionally spending energy on less significant connections when that energy should be channeled toward those who care about us and are invested in our well-being. Perhaps you have lost track of who is and is not close to you.

Perhaps you feel depleted after interacting with particular individuals, but you cannot explain why. It may be time for you to conduct a personal inventory. Consider your social life to be a dartboard comprised of concentric circles. The target reflects your most intimate personal relationships. Each ring out represents one step away from these intimate ties.

Time: 20 minutes

Format: Written exercise

Instructions:

Consider the social analysis dartboard, read the descriptions of each connection type, and then react to the questions.

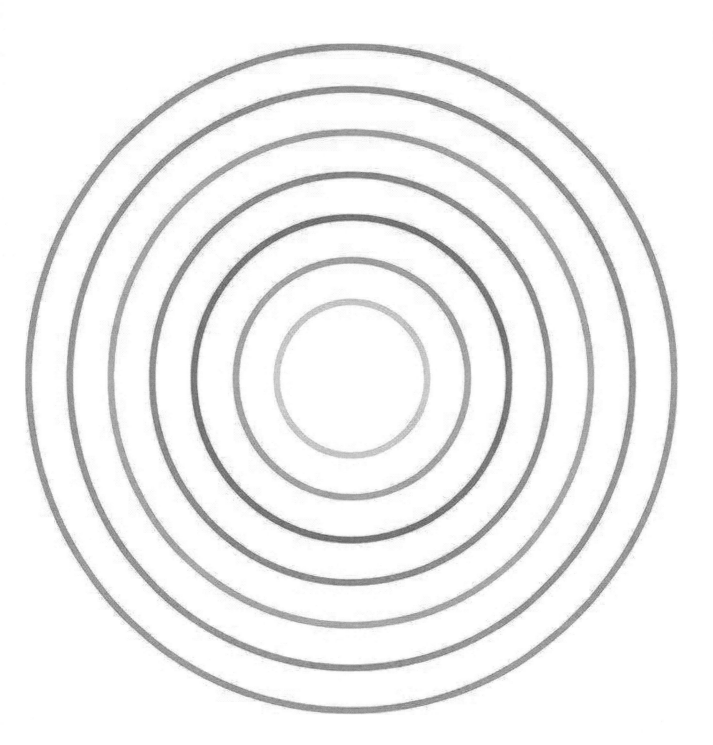

People with whom you can be transparent, a relatively limited number (perhaps nil) due to the high level of trust required.

You can tell practically anything to your closest friends, but you may withhold some personal information.

Close friends are those with whom you frequently spend time and are willing to reveal intimate parts of your life depending on who is there.

Friends are those with whom you attend events and participate in activities but with whom you reveal fewer intimate elements of your life.

Acquaintances are friendly individuals, such as coworkers and friends of friends.

Familiar faces are those you recognize and occasionally greet in the coffee shop and around town.

As of early 2021, about 8 billion people were on the planet.

1) Conduct an inventory. For each dartboard ring, name the persons in your life who fit that category. Use their names, as it is essential to be clear about who these individuals are. If you do not know the names of the " familiar faces," you can describe them.

Bull' s-eye:

_____

_____

_____

Best friends:

_____

_____

_____

Close friends:

_____

_____

_____

Friends:

_____

_____

_____

Acquaintances:

_____

_____

_____

Familiar faces:

_____

_____

_____

2. Determine the number of individuals in each category. Doing so allows you to consider where you may be lacking in friendships or whether you are focusing your energy on the correct individuals. For example, sometimes you may sense that there are not enough people in a ring, and sometimes you may feel that there are too many.

Recalibrate where you should put energy in various interactions; this raises awareness of your emotional investment and comprehension of how relationships function.

If you' ve selected individuals in your spheres that you want to draw closer or into your inner circle, write down some suggestions for how you might do so. It could be as simple as striking up a conversation with a familiar face at the coffee shop. It may also necessitate separating one' s self from " too close" others (i.e., in an inner circle and requiring more energy but with little or no payoff in return) .

MAKE AND NOTICE SMALL GESTURES

There are simple gestures that we show our friends, family, and people we regularly contact that tend to wane as the relationship progresses or as life gets busier. It is essential to maintain a pattern of kindness in partnerships so that both parties know they are appreciated.

If you observe any important relationship, whether with a friend, partner, coworker, or family member, is becoming strained or distant, take the time to do thoughtfully kind things for that person.

Time: 15 to 20 minutes

Format: Behavioral activity, observation, and written exercise

Instructions:

Extend a purposeful, friendly gesture. It might be as basic as sending a text message that says " Hello." People enjoy being remembered and praised. Also, take note when others make a friendly gesture toward you. If you observe that they are actively being kind, say something to reinforce their behavior. For example, if they are supportive, you could say, " I truly appreciate that you contacted me today to wish me luck on my meeting."

You are altering your behavior to be more supportive of others by reinforcing their positive behaviors and engaging in your own.

Respond to the prompts below:

List three things you used to do for a person that you no longer do but could do to strengthen your relationship.

1.

2.

3.

What activities is a person taking or has taken in the past to become your friend? Put them in writing. After identifying the activities, share them with the individual and express your appreciation for their behavior.

_____

_____

_____

5.5 IMPROVING SELF-ESTEEM

PRACTICE SELF-APPRECIATION

Redirecting your inner critic can be as simple as bringing your attention back to the things you like and respect. The more you love and accept yourself, the less weight your critical thoughts have over you.

The activity doesn't mean you won't ever have constructive judgments of yourself or your conduct; rather, your comments will be less stinging and more like suggestions than outright proclamations. Nevertheless, acknowledging and celebrating one's uniqueness and the blessings bestowed upon them is crucial in developing a sense of personal worth.

Instructions: Answer the following:

Listing even five positive qualities or experiences in your life will do, and you'll feel better just thinking about them. A simple " I like my eyes" might do the trick. You may also wish to laud a positive trait you possess, such as the conviction that " I am a caring person."

1. _____

2. _____

3. _____

4. _____

5. _____

Write down all the reasons you love these qualities in yourself. What is it about your eyes that you find so appealing? Do you have amazing eyesight? Do they have a special color that appeals to you? Are they deep or warm? Why does being helpful to other people make you feel good? Is it because you're kind to youngsters, the elderly, the animals, or those less fortunate? Generate as many justifications as possible for feeling gratitude toward those five items. Write as many reasons as you can.

_____

_____

_____

PRACTICE SELF-COMPASSION

When it comes to others, we are eager to show compassion, but when it comes to ourselves, we are far less forgiving. Kindness and compassion for yourself are great ways to boost your confidence. Self-compassion isn' t about wallowing in pity for yourself; it' s about recognizing the reality that you deserve to be comforted when you' re going through a tough period in life and that it hurts to be subjected to relentlessly critical internal monologue. With self-compassion in mind, you treat yourself with kindness no matter what.

Instead of trying to ignore or push away your bad emotions and ideas, you embrace them and then choose to treat yourself kindly. Like a good friend, you are kind and compassionate to yourself; to satisfy your desire for approval, practice self-compassion. It' s great when people care about you and want to help, but knowing that you can deal with your sorrow without anybody else' s approval is also empowering.

Instructions:

This technique can be done anywhere (even while walking down the street) and at any time during the day when you become aware of painful negative thoughts.

1. Be aware of your critical ideas. You might think, " I detest my life," for example. " There is absolutely nothing in my favor."

2. Take note of how you feel due to these thoughts.

3. Instead of convincing yourself that these beliefs are false, consider showing compassion. In addition, responding to these thoughts with a soft voice can be helpful, either out loud or internally.

"I' m sorry this is happening to you. You have been through a lot recently."

This phrase serves as a sobering reminder that your emotions are justified and that life is difficult. Recognizing the difficulty of a situation might help lessen some of the pain associated with it.

4. Consider how you feel after attempting this strategy multiple times.

HAVING A HEALTHY SELF-ESTEEM

When you have a healthy sense of who you are, you are less likely to get angry with yourself, you are less likely to take offense quickly, and you are more likely to see the best in other people. So look at this list of great traits and cross out the ones that apply to you.

If you' re struggling with this task, you may always ask a close friend or family member, " What are some qualities you enjoy about me?" Or you can speculate on their potential responses. It' s okay to treat yourself kindly once in a while. However, anger can only be overcome by first accepting one' s self. Remember that positive traits don' t necessarily apply to all situations and sectors of life; if you possess quality in one area, that quality is a part of who you are and should factor into how you feel about yourself.

If you are a hilarious person among your friends but find it difficult to be amusing in front of strangers, you should still mark " funny" off the list.

I am:

Smart

Creative

Funny

Good at/ with

Good at/ with

Honest

Kind

Humble

Friendly

Helpful

Good at my job

A good student

Driven

Strong

_____

_____

_____

Now put your adjectives and verbs into a sentence:

_____

_____

_____

Recite this affirmation out loud to yourself in the mirror. Then, use it as a source of inspiration whenever you need a lift on your path to better anger management.

_____

_____

_____

HEAR AND RESPOND TO YOUR INNER CRITIC

Your inner critic is a sometimes well-meaning part of your mind that wants the best for you. It offers advice or feedback on your character or the actions you take. However, sometimes it doesn't have the most sensitive or tactful approach. This exercise helps you regain your power and observe how your inner critic is trying to help.

Time: 15 to 20 minutes

Format: Observation and written exercise

Instructions:

Respond to the following prompts to discover how your inner critic is trying to help you:

1. Sit quietly for a moment and listen. Now, for the next five minutes, list all the thoughts your inner critic is throwing at you. They may come at you rapid-fire. Allow yourself to write down these thoughts without judging them or trying to stop them. These are *automatic thoughts*. (Some examples of automatic thoughts, which are not necessarily yours, might include criticisms like, "I'm bad with money," "I'm not a good friend," and "I'm a lazy parent.")

2. Now, review your list. These statements may sound pretty harsh. On the surface, it may seem like your inner critic is being cruel—Circle just three of the thoughts to work with for now. We'll call these your "hot" thoughts. Pick the three that seem to be the most bothersome of the bunch.

3. Look at these three hot thoughts without judging them and, in the spaces provided, try to reframe them, so they are helpful. To help you here, let's look at the three examples of automatic thoughts from step 1, with the understanding that these may not be your thoughts:

- "I'm bad with money." The inner critic tells you that you have some financial issues that need to be worked on. However, you can reframe this critical statement of "I'm bad with money" to "I need help with money management." For example, contact a financial advisor or ask someone you trust for help.

- "I'm not a good friend." Here, your inner critic tells you to focus on your friendships and work on them. By *labeling* yourself a "bad friend," you are learning that you care about improving your friendships. Now you can examine ways to show up for your friends while being gentle with yourself and recognizing that no friendship is perfect. For example, you may choose to write down one friend's name and think of something nice you can do for them. Maybe you'll send a text or call them and ask how they're doing.

- "I'm a lazy parent." Being a parent is difficult. Your inner critic recognizes that being a parent requires much hard work. However, there's a difference between being lazy and feeling tired. All parents get tired. You are calling yourself lazy because you care. That makes you a good parent. You may ask yourself, "What small thing can I do to show I care, despite feeling tired?"

Thought 1: _____

Reframe: _____

Thought 2: _____

Reframe: _____

Thought 3: _____

Reframe: _____

Do you see how your inner critic might be trying to help? The way it's communicating is harsh, but the message encourages you to better yourself. We all have challenges in life and things that we can get better at, and that's what the inner critic is trying to show us. You're not bad with money, a bad friend, or a lazy parent. But at the same time, there are always ways you can seek to feel better about yourself and improve your relationships.

GIVE YOUR INNER CRITIC TIME OFF WITH AN ACTIVITY

Not listening to your inner critic is an effective strategy for dealing with it. When you're inactive, you have more time to focus on your negative ideas, which makes self-criticism easier. Also, the more sedentary you are, the greater the likelihood and frequency of hearing your thoughts.

Conversely, it isn't easy to be self-critical when engaging in an activity that provides a sense of accomplishment or enjoyment. Some CBT exercises involve altering one's thinking, but science demonstrates that some activities can also improve one's mood. The term for this is behavioral activation.

Time: 30 minutes

Format: Written exercise and behavioral activity

Instructions: Choose a period each day to completely engage in an activity that you enjoy for its own sake, that offers you a sense of success when it's completed, or both! Activities include cooking, yoga, nature walks, a relaxing bath or shower, or handicraft. Also included are tasks such as cleaning, paying bills, and doing laundry. Try to be fully present in whatever activity you choose, observing how the food smells as you prepare, how your body feels as you hold a yoga position, or how the leaves sound as the wind blows through them. Consider how you feel after completion. Are you more motivated?

By engaging in meaningful activities, you can divert your focus away from the negative chatter in your thoughts and immerse yourself in life-enhancing experiences. The exercise can also be used to engage in life completely. And if you can complete this task, you will feel good about yourself, which will help you develop confidence, boost your self-esteem, and raise your motivation.

Respond to the prompts below:

_____

_____

_____

What activity do you wish to engage in?

_____

_____

_____

What days and times will you perform this task?

_____

_____

_____

Make a note of your feelings after engaging in the activity:

_____

_____

_____

After engaging in the activity, assess your degree of motivation from 0 (no motivation) to 10 (high motivation) .

O—O—O—O—O—O—O—O—O—O—O

0   1   2   3   4   5   6   7   8   9   10

CRAFT YOUR AFFIRMATIONS

If you' ve been depressed for a while, you' re undoubtedly used to hearing vicious thoughts about your personality, the world you live in, and your future. Developing and using affirmations is one technique to overcome negative thoughts. Affirmations are phrases or mantras that help combat negative ruminations directly.

Time: 10 minutes

Format: Written exercise and verbal practice

Instructions:

Use an affirmation that resonates with you and repeat it regularly when negative self-talk develops to divert your focus. Here is how to select one:

Consider something easy and clear you might say to a buddy experiencing difficulty, such as " You' re doing your best." Then, rephrase it to address yourself directly. Here are some suggestions:

- I am doing my best.

- My thoughts have no bearing on my value.

- I will simply concentrate on the task and take it one step at a time.

- I recognize that these assertions feel true, but sentiments are not facts.

Constructing a statement that connects with you is crucial, so experiment a bit with this. You may select multiple coping statements that address your ruminations. Try to generate three to five affirmations and record them here:

Note: It may also be beneficial to write your affirmation(s) on a post-it note and place it on your bathroom mirror or make it the wallpaper on your phone, or tablet, or computer.

PART 4: DIALECTIC BEHAVIORAL THERAPY

As a result of our innovative and non-traditional applications of Dialectical Behavior Therapy (DBT) , we felt compelled to document our methods in this book. However, we do not have extensive training in DBT and cannot provide clinical services in this area. The lack of requirements for when and how to provide DBT has allowed us to experiment with the model and shape it to fit our guiding principles, our client's unique needs, and the goals we' ve set together. Adapting DBT to the needs and constraints of the settings we serve is a direct result of our open thinking.

We have received criticism and praise for applying DBT in contexts where it was neither intended nor approved. We are fine with this debate. Despite our departure from the original DBT paradigm, we can perceive the positives in our current conceptual framework. All of our alterations have been deliberate and well-considered. When it is in the best interest of the client, we recommend them to a full-fidelity dialectical behavior therapy program. This situation happens when a client has a history of suicide ideation and requires the intensive treatment provided by a full-fidelity DBT program, preferably with access outside of traditional working hours.

Chapter 1: Definition of DBT

Dialectical Behavior Therapy (DBT) is "a form of CBT that emphasizes the importance of a collaborative relationship, support for the client, and the development of skills for dealing with highly emotional situations" (Psych Central, 2016) .It is in addition to the cognitive and behavioral aspects of treatment.

Originally developed to aid those with suicidal ideation, DBT has expanded to treat various disorders characterized by difficulties in managing one' s emotions. It has been successfully applied to treating substance abuse, eating disorders, and borderline personality disorder (Linehan Institute, n.d.) .

DBT could also be considered a form of CBT tailored to the needs of those who experience strong emotions. Mindfulness and emotional regulation are central tenets of Dialectical Behavior Therapy (DBT) as a form of Cognitive Behavior Therapy. Therefore, you may expect to gain tools for mindfulness, effective stress management, and better interpersonal connections from this course.

In the 1980s, Marsha M. Linehan, Ph.D., and her colleagues worked with people with Borderline Personality Disorder, which led to Dialectical Behavior Therapy (DBT) . Working with suicidal patients with Borderline Personality Disorder, Linehan realized that it is more effective to employ two opposing (dialectical) strategies: acceptance AND change, as opposed to cognitive behavior therapy (CBT) , which focuses primarily on detecting negative thought patterns and changing them to positive ones (change-focused) .

As a result, we have honed our methods for providing DBT in various contexts and to various client populations. This book will guide you as you tailor DBT to your needs while preserving its essential features. We practice Dialectical Behavior Therapy (DBT) skills such as mindfulness and acceptance of the current moment. As clinicians and supervisors, we have tried to incorporate the best parts of the traditional DBT model with our own experiences and insights; these include, perhaps most importantly, the lessons we have learned from our stumbles and blunders as well as the lessons our clients have taught us about tenacity, resilience, and grace.

We think DBT is consistent with the idea that we are imperfect and may grow from our experiences. Clinical staff and patients benefit from these features because they improve their quality of life and respond more effectively to adversity and emergencies.

Chapter 2: The Theory behind DBT

Dr. Marsha Linehan's " Cognitive-Behavioral Treatment of Borderline Personality Disorder and Skills Training Manual for Treating Borderline Personality Disorder" was published for the first time in 1993. (Linehan, 1993a; Linehan, 1993b) . This book was the first widely distributed text and skills manual for dialectical behavior therapy, while several publications on the topic had appeared in scholarly journals before this (DBT) . Since then, DBT has attracted the attention of scientists, medical professionals, and patients. Over a thousand articles and dozens of books have recently been written about this subject. Due to its efficacy with high-need, difficult clients, DBT has gained widespread attention.

Dr. Linehan developed DBT after realizing that existing methods were inadequate for working with clients who were suicidal regularly (Linehan 1993a; Linehan 1993b) . Acute care services, such as emergency rooms and hospital beds, were being overburdened by the dozens or hundreds of chronically suicidal clients in many places. As a result, they hated themselves and felt hopeless no matter how much counseling they went through or what psychiatric drugs they took.

The DBT paradigm has evolved from its origins as a manualized form of CBT into a widely applied therapy approach. DBT's overarching objective is to help people " create a life worth living," which can reduce destructive behavior, self-harm, and clinical symptoms, enhance relationships, raise functional levels, and boost happiness. Many integrated physicians now include DBT's framework and tools in their practice since it is compatible with other therapeutic modalities like cognitive behavioral therapy (CBT) .

Internal Experiences

DBT is predicated on the premise that people who suffer from BPD experience emotional turmoil (Linehan, 2015) . This clientele is highly attuned to their own and other's emotional states, and as a survival tactic, many have developed the ability to read the emotions of those around them. Although these customers' impressions of others aren't always true, they're usually close enough to act on those impressions. Customers rely on this skill to control their interactions with others and their actions. Clients with BPD are often accused of being manipulative because their actions are misinterpreted as an attempt to exert power over those around them. Clients with Borderline Personality Disorder may also accuse others of manipulation.

The therapeutic connection is especially sensitive to this problem, but it is problematic regardless of whether one or both parties intend to manipulate the other. Understanding this type of conduct and establishing healthy limits while showing compassion is crucial for physicians. In addition, clinicians must strike a " both/ and" dialectical balance between empathetic relationships and boundaries, as clients can often perceive how physicians feel about them.

Individuals with BPD often report tremendous emotions and find it difficult to return to a " normal" state. Whether joyful or negative, these customers experience their emotions more strongly than the ordinary person. On a scale from 1 to 10, these customers' emotions are often considered " off the chart." On a scale from 1 to 10, their level of emotion is more like an 11, 15, or 100. Furthermore, these customers may experience their feelings for a prolonged period. If the average individual without BPD takes 30 to 45 minutes to return to baseline from a certain emotional state, these clients may take hours, days, or even a week.

Adopting a DBT perspective and employing the skills it offers is helpful for clients with BPD because of the greater intensity, chaos, and difficulty of their internal experiences. These clients also benefit from the DBT perspective' s emphasis on the present moment, its emphasis on frustration tolerance, its emphasis on emotion regulation, and its emphasis on the efficacy of relationships.

EXTERNAL EXPERIENCES

Given the above, it is not surprising that people with BPD may have atypical experiences in their relationships and circumstances, given the client' s unique internal experience. These people are told by their loved ones and authorities that their way of thinking, talking, and acting is improper and that they need to change to be accepted. That completely disproves your claim. It is exceedingly unlikely, if not impossible, for these people to act in any way other than their natural selves when commanded to do so.

When a person exhibits distressing feelings and harmful actions, they are often subjected to punishment or abuse. Unfortunately, not just kids do it; adults can sometimes have episodes of " acting out" when they feel particularly vulnerable. When they lose control of their emotions, such as anger or sadness, they may act in unhealthy ways, like getting into fights or hurting themselves, drinking excessively, taking drugs, overeating, engaging in risky sexual behavior, gambling, or spending above their means. They don' t want assistance and don' t believe anything can help them control their feelings. They may even be defensive of their feelings and actions with an air of superiority or despair. That' s why it' s so easy for others to categorize their feelings and actions as excessive and mistreat them.

In addition, these customers often hear from their loved ones that their issues aren' t that serious and that they could simply discover answers if they put in the effort. Words like " get over it," " stop making it worse than it needs to be," " why aren' t you more like _____," " you need to be less like _____," and " stop being so dramatic" are common in the conversations these customers have with friends and family.

THE CUMULATIVE EFFECT OF INTERNAL AND EXTERNAL EXPERIENCES

Those internal and environmental events discussed above help explain why clients with BPD are the way they are. If these things had happened once or twice, it' s unlikely that they would have negatively affected their development. But instead, they have been mistreated, let down, and traumatized repeatedly. As a result, they haven' t been able to draw on their resources successfully.

Skills-based DBT is well-suited to helping people with BPD because it allows them to adapt their coping strategies to various situations and focuses on the four main areas where BPD sufferers experience the most difficulty. As a result, this approach can provide them with the tools they need to start again and create lives they like once again.

REALITY IS SUBJECTIVE

Invalidity is subjective, and the onus for determining it rests squarely on the reader. One person' s experience of invalidation may not be the same as another' s, and those who feel they have been victimized may be accused of exaggerating or lying about it. However, according to the DBT paradigm, everyone' s perspective is genuine.

When a client shares an experience that is vastly different from our own or seems implausible, we as clinicians need to try to comprehend what they are trying to convey. For example, is the customer claiming to be offended, disrespectful, or fearful for their safety? It is important to remember that the client' s experience and interpretation are valid, even if they differ from ours.

THE FIVE COMPONENTS OF DBT

SKILLS TRAINING

Skills Training provides techniques for dealing with emotional and physical strain at times of crisis. These methods help you develop better interpersonal skills and teach you to live in the present moment, which is all we can control because the past is gone and the future hasn' t arrived.

Skills training in the classic DBT paradigm typically takes place in a psychoeducational group therapy context, which is a very effective method of skill acquisition. Students learn and practice skills from each of the four skill modules through class-like sessions that include homework. However, skills can also be taught in individual sessions, phone support, and through outreach programs in the community.

Competency development provides individuals with the means to overcome adversity and adopt more constructive patterns of conduct. Instead of the problematic behavior, clients can use their acquired skills to cope, endure, and soothe themselves. Skills can also be taught as a preventative method—the regular practice of these skills helps manage stress and lessen the risk of problem behaviors happening in the first place.

Since proficiency is enhanced by repetition, individuals can benefit greatly from practicing their abilities regularly, especially before they are required. The more the skills are employed, the more likely they will become second nature to the individual and the more effortlessly accessible they' ll be when needed. Skills are meant to be used in ways that contribute to a life worth living, such as by fostering positive, supportive relationships and habits.

INDIVIDUAL THERAPY

Clients develop a desire to alter their behavior through individual therapy. However, adapting to and embracing change can be challenging and frustrating. The four-part change matrix below might help you weigh the pros and cons of making a change against maintaining the status quo, validating the client, and delving into what stands in the way of change by discussing the benefits of maintaining the status quo and the drawbacks of making changes. After all, if there were nothing good about the customer' s activity, the client wouldn' t be engaging in it. Similarly, they wouldn' t need DBT if there were nothing negative about their behavior.

As part of this investigation, it will be possible to determine the positive aspects of maintaining the status quo and whether these positive aspects may be addressed in other, healthier ways. Removal of impediments is also an integral element of this procedure. Impediments to transformation: Is the client interested in learning more? Do they require additional training? Should the procedure be divided into sub-steps? Should we try to alter our social networks to help?

Another part of individual therapy is assistance with the client's day-to-day and past challenges. The skills group does minimal processing to prevent clients from being mistakenly triggered and from obtaining reinforcement for undesirable conduct. Individual therapy is optimal for processing trauma and its many aftereffects. Individual therapy also effectively treats many other mental health disorders and addictions. Individual therapy may occur as frequently as four times per week in the standard DBT approach.

Phone Coaching

Phone-based coaching aids patients in transferring their therapeutic gains to real-world settings. When clients are faced with everyday pressures and emergencies, they can call their clinicians for help. They phone their therapists before acting out when they are prompted. The therapists then guide their clients through applying immediate skills for better stress management and detachment from problematic behavior triggers.

Coaching over the phone is a great tool for helping clients break problematic patterns and learn new, more helpful ones that can improve their quality of life and those around them. In addition, phone coaching is a terrific option for those who want constant access to expert advice.

Team consultation

When it comes to dialectical behavior therapy (DBT), a "team consultation" is the same thing as "group supervision" but with a slightly different format. The goal of this section is to encourage clinicians to stick with DBT over the long haul and maintain client contact. The goal is to raise everyone on the team to a higher level of expertise through group discussions, assigned reading, and case consultations. When doctors encounter difficulties with a client, issues during therapy, or countertransference, the consultation team is there to lend assistance and ensure responsibility. In addition, the clinician's team can help them keep their bearings and a dialectical perspective.

Each consultation team member is a trained DBT clinician who actively employs various strategies to maintain a positive outlook on their job and prevent burnout. In dialectical behavior therapy (DBT) , a nonjudgmental attitude is one of the most effective techniques for practitioners. It assists the team and clinician in determining if a behavior is troublesome or functional, and refrains from assigning moral value to the client or the clinician. Practitioners who use this DBT technique in their daily life report feeling significantly more resilient.

ANCILLARY TREATMENT

DBT' s fifth and final phase entails collaboration with the patient' s primary care physicians, other medical staff, and the patient' s social networks. Ancillary treatment entails informing those people and groups about the Dialectical Behavior Therapy (DBT) paradigm, addressing how the client uses DBT, and asking for their support. When possible, we' d like the support system to ignore less-than-healthy or immature behaviors while reinforcing the positive ones.

When clients take responsibility for their care, we should support them; when they act damaged or impaired, we should not. Healthcare providers are urged to maintain composure and prevent crises from worsening, and patients are urged not to be overmedicated with any drugs, especially opiates, benzodiazepines, and stimulants. To achieve the goals of this section, we plan to employ the " consulting with the client" technique by teaching patients and their families how to work together with medical staff and other resources.

GENERAL SKILLS IN DBT

Mindfulness

The development of mindfulness abilities is a key benefit of DBT.

Mindfulness enables one to concentrate on the present or " live in the now." Doing this helps you focus on what is occurring within you (your thoughts, feelings, sensations, and impulses) and tune in to what is occurring around you (what you see, hear, smell, and touch) nonjudgmentally.

In the middle of emotional suffering, mindfulness skills enable you to slow down and concentrate on employing good coping strategies. The method can also assist you in maintaining composure and avoiding negative thought patterns and impulsive conduct.

Exercise Example: Observe Mindfulness Skill

Concentrate on your breathing. Observe the feeling of inhaling and exhaling. Observe the rise and fall of your abdomen as you breathe.

Trauma Tolerance

Skills in stress tolerance help you accept yourself and your existing circumstances. DBT offers various crisis management skills, including

Distraction

Enhancing the present

Self-soothing

Considering the merits and downsides of not tolerating suffering

Distress Tolerance

Techniques for stress tolerance prepare you for high emotions and allow you to manage them with a more optimistic long-term outlook.

Sample Exercise: Taking Control of Your Body

Up and down the stairs, sprint. If you're inside, go outdoors. Get up from your seat and move around. But, again, the objective is to become distracted by letting your emotions follow your body.

Interpersonal Effectiveness

Interpersonal effectiveness enables you to become more assertive in a relationship (by expressing your wants and being able to say " no") while maintaining a happy and healthy relationship. In addition, you will learn to interact and listen more effectively, deal with difficult individuals, and respect yourself and others.

Sample Exercise: GIVE

Use the term GIVE to increase positive communication and relationships:

Gentle. Do not attack, threaten, or evaluate the Interest of others. Display interest by attentive listening (do not interrupt others) .

Validate. Recognize the other person's thoughts and emotions.

Easy. Attempt to adopt a relaxed attitude (smile often and be light-hearted)

Emotional Management

Emotion regulation enables more effective management of intense emotions. The abilities you acquire will assist you in recognizing, naming, and altering your emotions.

When you recognize and manage extreme negative emotions (such as anger) , you become less emotionally vulnerable and have more good emotional experiences.

Chapter 3: DBT Activities

3.1 Mindfulness

The Observer Meditation

The Observer Meditation examines why it is beneficial to detach from our internal thoughts and feelings; this is a crucial component of Acceptance and Commitment Therapy, a therapy in which mindfulness plays a significant role.

Adopting an Observer perspective can help us detach ourselves from problematic realms of life with which we may be overidentifying.

To begin the exercise, perform the following:

- Listen to the script in a comfortable seated position.

- Allow your body and mind to fall into place.

- Try letting go of your ideas and clearing your mind of their typical concerns.

- Attend initially to the room in which you are seated. As you sit, imagine yourself from the outside, exactly as an outsider would. Next, bring your focus inside to your skin.

- Try to feel your skin while seated on the chair.

- Try to visualize the shape your skin is forming as it comes into touch with the chair, transferring your focus to any physical feelings you may be experiencing. Then, as you experience each, acknowledge its existence before allowing your consciousness to let go of it and move on naturally.

If you have any feelings, acknowledge them and give them room. Then, return your focus to observing yourself; your emotions and thoughts are present, but you are distinct from them and witnessing them. This phrase is " Observe you."

You can continue this activity for as long as you choose, and there are other stages you can work through to become an observer of yourself. However, it is first challenging since we tend to overreact to and identify with our emotions.

The purpose of invoking the Observing Self is to enter a mode that permits you to take a step back from your own experiences and yourself. Nevertheless, you are simultaneously connecting with a deeper, emotionless self.

FIVE SENSES EXERCISE

This activity, known as the " five senses," guides quickly practicing mindfulness in almost any scenario. Simply observing something you are experiencing with each of your five senses is required.

Follow this sequence to exercise your Five Senses:

- Observe five visible items.

Observe your surroundings and identify five objects you can observe. Then, choose something typically overlooked, such as a shadow or a little fissure on the pavement.

- Note four things you can physically feel.

Bring consciousness to four things you are currently experiencing, such as the texture of your pants, the feeling of the breeze on your skin, or the smooth surface of the table on which your hands are resting.

- Consider three sounds you can hear.

Take a moment to listen and mentally note three background sounds. Doing this may include a bird' s chirp, the refrigerator' s hum, or the faint sounds of neighboring traffic.

- Observe two scents that you can detect.

Bring to the attention odors you normally ignore, whether pleasant or unpleasant. For example, the breeze may carry the scent of pine trees or a fast-food restaurant across the street if you are outside.

- Observe anything that you can taste.

Concentrate on one item you can taste at this very time. You can sip a beverage, chew gum, eat something, observe the current taste in your mouth, or even seek the air for a flavor by opening your lips.

This activity is a brief and relatively simple exercise for achieving mindfulness rapidly. If you have only a minute or two or don' t have the time or resources to perform a body scan or complete a worksheet, the five senses exercise can assist you or your clients quickly bringing consciousness to the present moment.

THE THREE-STEP MINDFULNESS WORKOUT

If you' re pressed for time, this 3-Step Mindfulness Worksheet contains an additional helpful activity. This exercise consists of only three steps:

1. First, remove yourself from " autopilot" and become conscious of what you are doing, thinking, and sensing in the present.

Try to halt and adopt a relaxed yet dignified stance. Recognize the thoughts and emotions that arise, but allow them to pass. Recognize who you are and your current condition.

2. Focus on the breath for six breaths or one minute.

The purpose is to concentrate on one thing: your breath. Be conscious of the movement of your body with each breath, including the rise and fall of your chest, the expansion and contraction of your abdomen, and the expansion and contraction of your lungs. Find your breath pattern and use this awareness to ground yourself in the present.

3. Spread consciousness outward, beginning with the body and the environment.

Permit the awareness to spread to the body. Become aware of your sensations, such as pains or tightness in your face or shoulders. Consider your body a complete vehicle for your inner self; if you choose, you can spread your consciousness to your surroundings. Focus on what is immediately in front of you. Observe the visible items' hues, contours, patterns, and textures. Focus your consciousness on the present moment and your surroundings.

When you are ready to conclude the exercise, slowly open your eyes and try to transfer this attentiveness into your daily life.

THE TECHNIQUE OF MINDFUL WALKING DOWN THE STREET

Our ability to observe our thoughts, feelings, and sensations without attempting to repair, hide, or solve them is a fundamental process that can be changed by mindfulness practice. This awareness allows for a choice between impulses and actions, which can assist in developing coping skills and positive behavior modification.

In the first part of this intervention, the facilitator assists the client in visualizing a situation in which they are walking along a familiar street when they notice a familiar face across the street. They wave, but the other individual does not answer and continues walking by them.

In the second step, the facilitator encourages the client's introspection by posing questions.

While you were picturing, were you aware of any of your thoughts?

Did you become aware of your feelings as you imagined?

In the third and final stage, the facilitator asks the client to reflect on the sequence of emotions and thoughts that arose, how this affects their behavior, whether the exercise was beneficial, and any closing remarks.

THE THREE-MINUTE BREATHING ROOM

Unlike meditations or a body scan, this exercise is fast and useful for launching a mindfulness practice.

With meditations and the body scan, thoughts frequently arise, making it difficult to maintain a calm and clear mind. This last activity may be the ideal strategy for individuals with hectic lives and minds. The exercise is divided into three stages, each lasting one minute, as follows:

The first minute is devoted to answering the question " How am I doing right now?" by focusing on the feelings, ideas, and sensations that occur and attempting to put them into words.

The second minute is spent maintaining breath awareness.

The final minute is devoted to expanding attention away from the breath and sensing how breathing affects the rest of the body.

Keeping one's mind still can be difficult, as thoughts frequently arise. The goal is not to prevent things from entering your thoughts but to let them enter and depart. Attempt to observe them.

3.2 Distress Tolerance

The STOP Skill

In a crisis, the STOP Skill is an excellent first-resort tool.

S – Stop!

Do not react to any impulses you may be experiencing. Maintain command of your emotions and physical body. Remain still.

T – Take a Step Back!

Take yourself out of the situation. Take a momentary pause or a deep breath. Do not behave rashly based on your emotions.

O – Observe!

Observe your surroundings and environment, both inside and outside. How do you feel? What are other people saying or doing?

P - Proceed with Caution!

Consider your situational objectives and behave with complete awareness. What can be done to improve the situation, and what actions will worsen it?

Pros and Cons

Create a list of the benefits and drawbacks of acting on your impulses. Indulging in dangerous, addictive, or harmful activities, giving in, giving up, or just avoiding what must be done are examples of acting on your impulses. Make a separate list of the advantages and disadvantages of resisting these desires.

Carry the list with you and consult it frequently. Refer to your list when a crisis or impulse for impulsive action develops. Consider what transpired in the past when you acted in response to your crisis urges. Use your pros and cons list to choose a different course of action this time.

DISTRACTING WITH A WISE MIND: ACCEPTS

Sometimes, the best way to get through a crisis is to temporarily divert your attention away from the issue. Doing this permits us to temporarily move away and return to whatever task or crisis we face with renewed vigor. But, first, it is essential to realize a significant difference between temporarily distracting yourself and regularly avoiding an issue over a longer period, which could worsen things.

There are several methods for diverting attention available. They can be remembered using the acronym ACCEPTS.

A - Activities: Watch an episode of your favorite Netflix show, walk or engage in physical activity, play video games, clean a room or part of your home, spend time with a friend or family, read a book, or finish a puzzle.

C – Contributions: Sign up to perform some volunteer work. Assist a friend or relative with a project. Donate stuff you no longer need, or simply do something kind for another person, such as offering words of encouragement or a hug.

C - Comparisons: Compare how you feel now to how you felt in the past. Consider how fortunate you are and the various others around the globe who may be experiencing the same condition.

E - Emotions: Read a book about emotions. Watch a dramatic film. Listen to a song or album that is powerful. It could be any variety of emotions. Watch a horror film, a comedy, or listen to some soothing music.

P - Pushing away: Whatever the circumstance, simply set it aside for the time being. Deny the problem momentarily. Refuse to consider painful thoughts or images and block them out of your head.

T - Thoughts: Count things, whether ten or the number of flowers in a vase. Repeat the lyrics of your favorite song or view or read anything thought-provoking.

S - Sensations: Crush that stress ball. Take a shower, hot or cold. Or play some extremely loud music.

FIVE-SENSE SELF-SOOTHING

Concentrating on your five senses diverts your attention from the uncomfortable circumstance to something completely different. In a crisis, this brief respite helps you reconnect with your whole self and the world around you.

Vision: Provide your eyes with stimulation. You can observe people or go window shopping. You can start a fire or light a candle to engulf the flame. You might visit a park to take in the sights of nature. Observe the sunset or dawn, or view some artwork.

Go outside and listen to the leaves blowing in the breeze, the water running through a stream, or city traffic. Take note of the humming of an air conditioner, or grab your musical instrument of choice for a quick jam session.

Burn some incense or a scented candle to provide fragrance. Create a window. Take a bath with your preferred soaps, or apply your preferred perfume or cologne.

Consume your preferred dish or brew a calming cup of tea. Chew some gum or consume some butterscotch candy. Focus on savoring each meal item individually, regardless of your selection.

Pet your pet dog or cat. Relax in a plush chair. Take a bath or wrap yourself in your favorite blanket.

Remember to observe the calming sensation of whatever you are touching.

IMPROVE the PRESENT

IMPROVE is another effective DBT distress tolerance technique that aids in crisis confrontation.

I - Imagery: Use your imagination to create a peaceful atmosphere or decorate a room where nothing can harm you. Create a relaxing environment of imagination or relive a good memory moment by moment.

M - Meaning: In a terrible time, seek the underlying meaning. Concentrate and repeat in your mind the positive features.

Prayer: Open your heart to a superior being, God, or your Wise Mind. Pray for courage and have faith in God or another higher power.

R - Relaxation: Unwind in a hot tub. Perform yoga or stretching. Inhale deeply. Facial muscles must be relaxed.

O - One thing in the present: Remain in the present by focusing all your attention on the task at hand.

V - Vacation: Allow yourself a brief break. Jump into bed and cover your head with the sheets. Spend a day at the beach, in the woods, on the lake, or by the river. Turn off your phone and spend the entire afternoon in a park.

E - Encouragement and Reconsideration: Be your own greatest cheerleader. Consider or utter phrases such as " You' ve got this," " I' ll be OK," and " You' re the man!"

3.3 Interpersonal Effectiveness

Skills Assessment Handout

Before attempting to develop your interpersonal communication abilities, it is prudent to assess your present level of proficiency with each.

You are instructed to rate yourself on a scale from 1 to 5 for each ability, using the following rubric:

1 – I am terrible at that ability

2 – I am impoverished

3 – I am occasionally good

4 – I am typically good

5 – I am always good

By averaging your evaluations, you can calculate an overall ranking for your " interpersonal effectiveness" talent, but the individual ratings are also valuable.

To improve your communication skills, you must first establish a baseline. If you have a benchmark against which to measure progress, it is much easier to detect changes!

Try To Hear Nothing Activity

In this entertaining and potentially enlightening activity, group members will have the opportunity to demonstrate their acting skills.

For this activity, the group must be divided into pairs. In each pair, one person should speak first while the other " listens," and then the roles should be reversed.

The first speaker (Partner A) is asked to speak for two minutes straight on any topic of their choosing. After that, partner B must make it evident that they are not listening to Partner A while Partner A is speaking.

Partner B cannot speak and must rely on body language to convey their message to Partner A.

Partner A has two minutes to speak, followed by two minutes for Partner B while Partner A " listens."

The group will likely find it difficult to continue speaking while their spouse is not listening! This realization is a fundamental takeaway from the activity: body language plays a crucial role in communication, and listeners substantially impact how the encounter unfolds in addition to those speaking.

After each group member has spoken and " listened" in turn, each individual should record their instant reactions to having a speaking partner who is not listening.

They will likely experience emotions like:

I felt frustrated.

I was furious.

I believed I was unimportant.

I believed that what I was saying was dull.

I couldn' t keep talking.

I felt insignificant and irrelevant.

Next, group members should take note of the actions their partner exhibited that indicated they were not listening, such as:

- Away, with the head bowed toward the ground or tilted to the side
- not making eye contact
- Observing the floor/ ceiling
- Crossed arms and legs

- a face devoid of expression

- Activity is incompatible with active listening, such as yawning, whistling, or itching.

- Preoccupation (observing one' s environment, phone, etc.)

- No contact whatsoever

Even though this exercise is an exaggeration of what it is like to speak to someone who is not listening, it might help folks who are not very observant or have low social skills evaluate their conduct while engaging with others.

It' s simple to decide to practice active listening in your conversations. Still, it' s more difficult to remember all of the target behaviors (as well as all of the non-target behaviors) . This exercise will assist participants in recognizing and remembering the characteristics of a good listener.

SABOTAGE EXERCISE

Sabotage Exercise is another enjoyable activity involving negative interpersonal actions to highlight the positive alternatives.

This activity should be performed in a group sufficiently sized to divide into at least two or three groups of four to five individuals.

Instruct each group to spend approximately ten minutes brainstorming, discussing, and listing all the possible ways to sabotage a group assignment. Anything they can come up with is fair game; it only needs to be sufficiently disruptive to derail a team' s mission.

Once each group has compiled a substantial list of ways to sabotage a group assignment, compare responses in the larger group. Put all of them on the chalkboard, whiteboard, or flip board at the front of the room.

Then, reform the groups and direct them to create a five- to ten-point contract outlining agreed-upon standards for productive group work. Group members should glean excellent ideas from the sabotage ideas (i.e., what to do (or not to do) for successful group work) .

For instance, if a group listed " do not communicate with any other group members" as a technique to sabotage the group assignment, they might come up with " talk with other group members frequently" as a guideline for productive group work.

This exercise will assist participants in understanding what makes for a positive group experience while simultaneously providing them with the opportunity to have a positive group experience.

Strengths and Weaknesses of the Group

When it comes to achieving tasks, groups have a significant advantage over individuals in that they may compensate for individuals' flaws, complement their strengths, and provide balance to the group.

In this exercise, group members will engage in critical thinking and debate their strengths and shortcomings, as well as those of their fellow group members and the group as a whole.

Instruct the group to consider each member's strengths and weaknesses as part of this exercise. Please encourage them to be candid yet courteous, especially when acknowledging their weaknesses.

Once each team has compiled a thorough inventory of the strengths and shortcomings of each group member, they should consider how these attributes may affect group dynamics. For example, which characteristics will positively affect group interactions? What shortcomings have the potential to disrupt group interactions?

Finally, have each team discuss the ideal team composition. For example, is it preferable to have members with similar traits or a wide variety of personalities, talents, and abilities? What are the benefits and drawbacks of each team type?

This debate will encourage participants to think critically about what constitutes a productive team, how different personalities interact, and how to adapt one's conduct, group norms, and expectations to the varying personalities and skills of others.

Count the Squares

This game encourages group engagement and communication in a fun and engaging manner.

All that is required is this image (or a similar image of several squares) placed on a PowerPoint presentation or the front wall or board.

In the first phase, allow each group member a few minutes to count the number of squares in the diagram and record their answer. They should complete this task in silence.

Next, have each group member announce how many squares they counted. Put these on the whiteboard.

Instruct each participant to select a partner and count the squares once more. They may only communicate with each other when determining the number of squares.

Upon completion, have each pair share their number once again.

Instruct the participants to count the squares once more in groups of four to five individuals. When they are completed, re-record the numbers each group has tallied.

Almost definitely, at least one group will have correctly counted forty squares. Next, have this group explain to the remaining participants how they reached 40.

Finally, lead the entire group in a discussion about group synergy and why the count (presumably) kept moving closer and closer to 40 as more people joined forces to solve the challenge.

Participants will understand the significance of effective group communication, gain experience working in pairs and groups, and perhaps enjoy themselves while performing this exercise.

GAME OF NON-VERBAL INTRODUCTION

The objective of this game is to meet new individuals and introduce them to the rest of the group.

You should schedule this game on the first day of group therapy, training, or any other activity to introduce each participant.

Pair up the group members with the individual seated next to them. Tell them to introduce themselves and to include something fascinating or uncommon about themselves in their introductions.

Once each pair has been introduced and has learned something fascinating about the other, return attention to the broader group.

Inform the group members that they must each introduce their partner to the group without using words or props. Instead, each partner must solely use actions to introduce the other.

This game is not only a terrific icebreaker for introducing individuals to one another but also a fun method for group members to see the value of verbal communication (something they may only realize when they cannot use it!) and the significance of nonverbal communication.

If you have the time, you can conduct a group discussion on nonverbal communication, the signs we pick up from other people' s behavior, and the importance of receiving feedback from those with whom you communicate.

3.4 Emotion Regulation

STOPP

If you struggle to regulate your emotions, think about how to STOP (Vivyan, 2015) .

STOPP is a tactic that will help you deal with overwhelming emotions in the heat of the moment. It combines cognitive behavioral therapy (CBT) , dialectical behavior therapy (DBT) , and mindfulness meditation to help you successfully confront and manage your emotional response to a stressful, difficult, or anger-inducing experience.

STOPP stands for:

S – Stop!

Please wait a moment.

T - Take a Breath.

Become aware of your breathing as you inhale and exhale.

O – Observe

What thoughts are currently running through your mind?

Where is your concentration?

To what are you responding?

What bodily feelings do you observe?

P – Provide Some Context - Step Back

What is the larger context?

Consider the situation from a bird' s eye perspective;

What are alternative perspectives on this circumstance?

What would a dependable buddy say to me at this moment?

Is this thought factual or subjective?

What is a more plausible justification?

How crucial is this?

How significant will it be in six months?

P – Proceed.

What is the best action to take at this time? For me? For the benefit of others? For the circumstance?

What actions align with my values?

Carry out what is effective and proper.

If you just master one skill that can help you regulate your emotions more efficiently, it should be this one. One of the most essential and life-altering talents a person can acquire is the ability to pause between an acute emotional reaction and the following behaviors. You will be in an excellent position to manage your most difficult emotions if you practice STOPPING.

CONTRARY ACTION

The first ability is Opposite Action, which can be used to halt an extreme or highly charged feeling.

Typically, emotions accompany a certain behavior, such as disputes following rage or withdrawal following melancholy. However, we frequently presume that the relationship runs in the opposite direction, from emotion to behavior.

It is feasible to evoke a certain mood by engaging in an activity associated with that emotion.

Try doing the opposite of what you normally do when experiencing a certain emotion. For example, try speaking softly instead of shouting when you' re angry. Likewise, try conversing with friends instead of withdrawing from them when you are down.

VERIFY THE FACTS

It might be simple to exaggerate the significance of a situation or your feelings.

This technique will enable you to recognize this scenario occurring and lower your emotions' intensity.

157

To " verify the facts," pose yourself the following queries:

What occasion caused my emotion?

What assumptions and interpretations am I making about the event?

Do my feelings and their strength correspond to the situation? Or does it simply confirm my presumptions about the situation?

P.L.E.A.S.E.

The P.LE.A.S.E. talent recognizes the connection between the body and the brain. If you also manage your health and physique, you will likely find it much simpler to regulate your emotions.

Remember the following:

PL – Treat Physical Illness;

E – Eat a Healthy Diet;

A – Avoid Mood-Altering Substances;

S – Sleep Well;

E – Exercise.

Follow these tips to maintain a healthy and happy body, making it simpler to maintain a healthy and happy mind.

ATTEND TO POSITIVE OCCURRENCES.

Humans are remarkably adept at ignoring the positive and concentrating on the negative. It is normal, but not helpful!

If you discover you are focusing excessively on the negative, halt and shift your attention to the positive.

You can practice by engaging in one modest, positive activity daily and focusing on the positive aspects of that activity. Ignore little concerns and focus on pleasure, enjoyment, and fun!

Some examples of tiny, beneficial actions include:

- Have a decent, unhurried meal;

- Watch a movie;

- Visit with friends or family;

- Visit a local site such as a zoo or museum;

- Go for a walk;

- Put on headphones and listen to nothing but music.

- Have a picnic;

- Spend a night resting at home;

- Take up a new hobby.

CONCLUSION

Knowing what play therapy is, how it can help your teenager, and why it may be so effective will help you make the best decisions for them. Although play therapy is most commonly utilized with teens, it has also been shown to be effective in helping adults overcome issues, including trauma and its aftereffects and mood disorders. In the end, this treatment method will help any teen struggling mentally. Anxiety, depression, attention deficit hyperactivity disorder (ADHD) , post-traumatic stress disorder (PTSD) , trauma symptoms, attachment difficulties, and dissociation are all common mental health issues treated with play-based therapies.

A skilled play therapist will amass a toolkit of approaches throughout their career and use those approaches to address the varying requirements of their clientele. To prepare for YOUR work with your kids, you might need to learn from field experts, read countless books and articles, and participate in various training and classes. Yet, despite this extensive training in play therapy, you will discover that many of the most effective strategies were conceived on the fly during sessions, often by your teens themselves. Simply put, play therapy has a virtually endless supply of resources at its disposal.

Nevertheless, the book's resources are united by a similar denominator: they are all based on a model that prioritizes the needs of teenagers. As a result, the teen is the focal point of their attention. Teenagers get a sense of agency they may lack in other contexts when they participate in a reciprocal interaction. It's a unique aspect of the therapeutic relationship that helps teens feel safe enough to take care of themselves at the moment.

Because of their common effects, many people have both anxiety and sleeplessness. Anxiety can make it hard to fall asleep, and a lack of sleep can amplify anxiety. We discovered the physiological causes of anxiety and sleeplessness and how Cognitive Behavioral Therapy (CBT) can be used to alter one's outlook on life and make positive changes that lead to better sleep.

If the methods outlined in this book produce results for you, keep employing them. Also, remember that this is a slow procedure that will provide results. The time it takes to alter neural pathways and modify routines for better sleep highly depends on the participant's dedication to the program. The initial step in any faith journey can seem daunting, but remember the words of Dr. Martin Luther King, Jr.: " You can take the first step even if you can't see the full staircase."

Congratulations on Starting to Heal!

REFERENCES

Barlow, D. (2022) . *Inner Child Recovery Work with Radical Self Compassion, Self-Control Practices, and Emotional Intelligence: From Conflict to Resolution for Better Relationships.* ROADTOTRANQUILITY™.

Cathy Moonshine, P. M.-I.-I. (2019) . *Dialectical Behavior Therapy: The Clinician's Guidebook for Acquiring Competency in DBT* (Vol. I) . Eau Claire, WI: PESI Publishing & Media.

Felman, A. (2020, January 11) . *What to know about anxiety.* Retrieved June 6, 2022, from MedicalNewsToday: https: / / www.medicalnewstoday.com/ articles/ 323454

Gillihan, S. J. (2018) . *Cognitive Behavioural Therapy Made Simple: 10 Strategies for Managing Anxiety, Depression, Anger, Panic, and Worry.* Althea Press.

Gruzewski, K. (2020) . *Therapy Games for Teens: 150 Activities to Improve Self-Esteem, Communication, and Coping Skills.* Emeryville, California: Rockridge Press.

Huang, B. (2021) . *DBT Workbook for Adults: Develop Emotional Wellbeing with Practical Exercises for Managing Fear, Stress, Worry, Anxiety, Panic Attacks, Intrusive Thoughts & More.*

Jennie Marie Battistin, M. L. (2019) . *Mindfulness for Teens: Exercises to Feel Calm, Stay Focused & be Your Best Self in 10 Minutes a Day.* Emeryville, California: Rockridge Press.

Leah Guzman, A.-B. (2020) . *Essential Art Therapy Exercises: Effective Techniques to Manage Anxiety, Depression, and PTSD.* Emeryville, California: Rockridge Press.

Linehan, M. M. (2015) . *DBT Skills Training: Handouts and Worksheets.* New York, NY: The Guilford Press.

Megan Maccutcheon, L. (2019) . *The Ultimate Self-Esteem Workbook for Teens: Overcome Insecurity, Defeat your Inner Critic, and Live Confidently.* Emeryville, California: Rockridge Press.

Nixaly Leonard, L. (2022) . *The CBT Workbook for Anger Management: Evidence-Based Exercises to Help you Understand your Triggers and Take Charge of Your Emotions.* Oakland, California: Rockridge Press.

Simon A. Rego, P. D. (2021) . *The CBT Workbook for Mental Health: Evidence-Based Exercises to Transform Negative Thought and Manage Your Well-Being.* Emeryville, California: Rockridge Press.

Telford, O. (2020) . *Cognitive Behavioural Therapy: Simple Techniques to Instantly Overcome Depression, Relieve Anxiety, and Rewire Your Brain.*

Tiffany Loggins, P. (2022) . *CBT WorkBook for Therapists Essential Cognitive Behavioural Therapy Strategies to Treat Mental Health.* Oakland, California: Rockridge Press.

Made in the USA
Las Vegas, NV
09 October 2023

78774852R00092